Service Applications
Complete Self-Assessment Guide

The guidance in this Self-Assessment is based on Service Application best practices and standards in business process architecture, design and quality management. The guidance is also based on the professional judgment of the individual collaborators listed in the Acknowledgments.

Notice of rights

Trademarks

Table of Contents

About The Art of Service

The Art of Service, Business Process Architects since 2000, is dedicated to helping stakeholders achieve excellence.

Defining, designing, creating, and implementing a process to solve a stakeholders challenge or meet an objective is the most valuable role… In EVERY group, company, organization and department.

Unless you're talking a one-time, single-use project, there should be a process. Whether that process is managed and implemented by humans, AI, or a combination of the two, it needs to be designed by someone with a complex enough perspective to ask the right questions.

Someone capable of asking the right questions and step back and say, 'What are we really trying to accomplish here? And is there a different way to look at it?'

With The Art of Service's Standard Requirements Self-Assessments, we empower people who can do just that — whether their title is marketer, entrepreneur, manager, salesperson, consultant, Business Process Manager, executive assistant, IT Manager, CIO etc... —they are the people who rule the future. They are people who watch the process as it happens, and ask the right questions to make the process work better.

Contact us when you need any support with this Self-Assessment and any help with templates, blue-prints and examples of standard documents you might need:

http://theartofservice.com
service@theartofservice.com

Included Resources - how to access

Included with your purchase of the book is the Service

Applications Self-Assessment Spreadsheet Dashboard which contains all questions and Self-Assessment areas and auto-generates insights, graphs, and project RACI planning - all with examples to get you started right away.

How? Simply send an email to
access@theartofservice.com
with this books' title in the subject to get the Service Applications Self Assessment Tool right away.

You will receive the following contents with New and Updated specific criteria:

- The latest quick edition of the book in PDF

- The latest complete edition of the book in PDF, which criteria correspond to the criteria in...

- The Self-Assessment Excel Dashboard, and...

- Example pre-filled Self-Assessment Excel Dashboard to get familiar with results generation

- In-depth specific Checklists covering the topic

- Project management checklists and templates to assist with implementation

INCLUDES LIFETIME SELF ASSESSMENT UPDATES

Every self assessment comes with Lifetime Updates and Lifetime Free Updated Books. Lifetime Updates is an industry-first feature which allows you to receive verified self assessment updates, ensuring you always have the most accurate information at your fingertips.

Get it now- you will be glad you did - do it now, before you forget.

Send an email to **access@theartofservice.com** with this books' title in the subject to get the Service Applications Self Assessment Tool right away.

Purpose of this Self-Assessment

This Self-Assessment has been developed to improve understanding of the requirements and elements of Service Applications, based on best practices and standards in business process architecture, design and quality management.

It is designed to allow for a rapid Self-Assessment to determine how closely existing management practices and procedures correspond to the elements of the Self-Assessment.

The criteria of requirements and elements of Service Applications have been rephrased in the format of a Self-Assessment questionnaire, with a seven-criterion scoring system, as explained in this document.

In this format, even with limited background knowledge of Service Applications, a manager can quickly review existing operations to determine how they measure up to the standards. This in turn can serve as the starting point of a 'gap analysis' to identify management tools or system elements that might usefully be implemented in the organization to help improve overall performance.

How to use the Self-Assessment

On the following pages are a series of questions to identify to what extent your Service Applications initiative is complete in comparison to the requirements set in standards.

To facilitate answering the questions, there is a space in front of each question to enter a score on a scale of '1' to '5'.

1 Strongly Disagree

2 Disagree

3 Neutral

4 Agree

5 Strongly Agree

Read the question and rate it with the following in front of mind:

'In my belief, the answer to this question is clearly defined'.

There are two ways in which you can choose to interpret this statement;
1. how aware are you that the answer to the question is clearly defined
2. for more in-depth analysis you can choose to gather evidence and confirm the answer to the question. This obviously will take more time, most Self-Assessment users opt for the first way to interpret the question and dig deeper later on based on the outcome of the overall Self-Assessment.

A score of '1' would mean that the answer is not clear at all, where a '5' would mean the answer is crystal clear and defined. Leave emtpy when the question is not applicable or you don't want to answer it, you can skip it without affecting your score. Write your score in the space provided.

After you have responded to all the appropriate statements in each section, compute your average score for that section, using the formula provided, and round to the nearest tenth. Then transfer to the corresponding spoke in the Service Applications Scorecard on the second next page of the Self-Assessment.

Your completed Service Applications Scorecard will give you a clear presentation of which Service Applications areas need attention.

Service Applications
Scorecard Example

Example of how the finalized Scorecard can look like:

Service Applications Scorecard

Your Scores:

BEGINNING OF THE SELF-ASSESSMENT:

CRITERION #1: RECOGNIZE

INTENT: Be aware of the need for change. Recognize that there is an unfavorable variation, problem or symptom.

In my belief, the answer to this question is clearly defined:

5 Strongly Agree

4 Agree

3 Neutral

2 Disagree

1 Strongly Disagree

1. What is the smallest subset of the problem you can usefully solve?
<--- Score

2. How do you take a forward-looking perspective in identifying Service Applications research related to market response and models?
<--- Score

3. What needs to stay?
<--- Score

4. What are the stakeholder objectives to be achieved with Service Applications?
<--- Score

5. Consider your own Service Applications project, what types of organizational problems do you think might be causing or affecting your problem, based on the work done so far?
<--- Score

6. Are there any specific expectations or concerns about the Service Applications team, Service Applications itself?
<--- Score

7. Are you dealing with any of the same issues today as yesterday? What can you do about this?
<--- Score

8. What activities does the governance board need to consider?
<--- Score

9. How are the Service Applications's objectives aligned to the group's overall stakeholder strategy?
<--- Score

10. Are there Service Applications problems defined?
<--- Score

11. Do you know what you need to know about Service Applications?
<--- Score

12. What are the expected benefits of Service Applications to the stakeholder?
<--- Score

13. Does Service Applications create potential expectations in other areas that need to be recognized and considered?
<--- Score

14. Will Service Applications deliverables need to be tested and, if so, by whom?
<--- Score

15. What are the clients issues and concerns?
<--- Score

16. Are losses recognized in a timely manner?
<--- Score

17. How do you recognize an Service Applications objection?
<--- Score

18. Do you need different information or graphics?
<--- Score

19. Who are your key stakeholders who need to sign off?
<--- Score

20. How does it fit into your organizational needs and tasks?
<--- Score

21. Why the need?

<--- Score

22. What Service Applications events should you attend?
<--- Score

23. What is the problem and/or vulnerability?
<--- Score

24. Why is this needed?
<--- Score

25. Think about the people you identified for your Service Applications project and the project responsibilities you would assign to them, what kind of training do you think they would need to perform these responsibilities effectively?
<--- Score

26. What prevents you from making the changes you know will make you a more effective Service Applications leader?
<--- Score

27. What are the minority interests and what amount of minority interests can be recognized?
<--- Score

28. What do employees need in the short term?
<--- Score

29. Which information does the Service Applications business case need to include?
<--- Score

30. Are employees recognized for desired behaviors?

<--- Score

31. As a sponsor, customer or management, how important is it to meet goals, objectives?
<--- Score

32. What should be considered when identifying available resources, constraints, and deadlines?
<--- Score

33. Who else hopes to benefit from it?
<--- Score

34. Will it solve real problems?
<--- Score

35. Can management personnel recognize the monetary benefit of Service Applications?
<--- Score

36. Are employees recognized or rewarded for performance that demonstrates the highest levels of integrity?
<--- Score

37. What else needs to be measured?
<--- Score

38. What is the Service Applications problem definition? What do you need to resolve?
<--- Score

39. What is the recognized need?
<--- Score

40. Who needs to know about Service Applications?

<--- Score

41. Where is training needed?
<--- Score

42. Who needs what information?
<--- Score

43. Who needs budgets?
<--- Score

44. What Service Applications problem should be solved?
<--- Score

45. Whom do you really need or want to serve?
<--- Score

46. What information do users need?
<--- Score

47. Who should resolve the Service Applications issues?
<--- Score

48. How do you assess your Service Applications workforce capability and capacity needs, including skills, competencies, and staffing levels?
<--- Score

49. What creative shifts do you need to take?
<--- Score

50. Are there recognized Service Applications problems?
<--- Score

51. How can auditing be a preventative security measure?
<--- Score

52. To what extent would your organization benefit from being recognized as a award recipient?
<--- Score

53. What does Service Applications success mean to the stakeholders?
<--- Score

54. Do you have/need 24-hour access to key personnel?
<--- Score

55. What Service Applications capabilities do you need?
<--- Score

56. Are problem definition and motivation clearly presented?
<--- Score

57. Which issues are too important to ignore?
<--- Score

58. What are the timeframes required to resolve each of the issues/problems?
<--- Score

59. What needs to be done?
<--- Score

60. How are training requirements identified?

<--- Score

61. Looking at each person individually – does every one have the qualities which are needed to work in this group?
<--- Score

62. What problems are you facing and how do you consider Service Applications will circumvent those obstacles?
<--- Score

63. Have you identified your Service Applications key performance indicators?
<--- Score

64. How do you identify the kinds of information that you will need?
<--- Score

65. What vendors make products that address the Service Applications needs?
<--- Score

66. To what extent does each concerned units management team recognize Service Applications as an effective investment?
<--- Score

67. Who needs to know?
<--- Score

68. Is it needed?
<--- Score

69. What tools and technologies are needed for a

custom Service Applications project?

<--- Score

70. Are there regulatory / compliance issues?

<--- Score

71. Is it clear when you think of the day ahead of you what activities and tasks you need to complete?

<--- Score

72. What is the extent or complexity of the Service Applications problem?

<--- Score

73. Who defines the rules in relation to any given issue?

<--- Score

74. What extra resources will you need?

<--- Score

75. Which needs are not included or involved?

<--- Score

76. Would you recognize a threat from the inside?

<--- Score

77. How much are sponsors, customers, partners, stakeholders involved in Service Applications? In other words, what are the risks, if Service Applications does not deliver successfully?

<--- Score

78. Is the quality assurance team identified?

<--- Score

79. Where do you need to exercise leadership?
<--- Score

80. Are controls defined to recognize and contain problems?
<--- Score

81. What are the Service Applications resources needed?
<--- Score

82. What do you need to start doing?
<--- Score

83. Are your goals realistic? Do you need to redefine your problem? Perhaps the problem has changed or maybe you have reached your goal and need to set a new one?
<--- Score

84. Do you need to avoid or amend any Service Applications activities?
<--- Score

85. Are there any revenue recognition issues?
<--- Score

86. How are you going to measure success?
<--- Score

87. Will a response program recognize when a crisis occurs and provide some level of response?
<--- Score

88. For your Service Applications project, identify and describe the business environment, is there more

than one layer to the business environment?
<--- Score

89. Does your organization need more Service Applications education?
<--- Score

90. What training and capacity building actions are needed to implement proposed reforms?
<--- Score

91. What would happen if Service Applications weren't done?
<--- Score

92. Do you recognize Service Applications achievements?
<--- Score

93. What Service Applications coordination do you need?
<--- Score

94. What are your needs in relation to Service Applications skills, labor, equipment, and markets?
<--- Score

95. Does the problem have ethical dimensions?
<--- Score

96. What resources or support might you need?
<--- Score

97. How do you recognize an objection?
<--- Score

98. Is the need for organizational change recognized?
<--- Score

99. Will new equipment/products be required to facilitate Service Applications delivery, for example is new software needed?
<--- Score

100. Did you miss any major Service Applications issues?
<--- Score

101. How many trainings, in total, are needed?
<--- Score

102. What situation(s) led to this Service Applications Self Assessment?
<--- Score

Add up total points for this section:
_ _ _ _ _ = Total points for this section

Divided by: _ _ _ _ _ _ (number of statements answered) = _ _ _ _ _ _
Average score for this section

Transfer your score to the Service Applications Index at the beginning of the Self-Assessment.

CRITERION #2: DEFINE:

INTENT: Formulate the stakeholder problem. Define the problem, needs and objectives.

In my belief, the answer to this question is clearly defined:

5 Strongly Agree

4 Agree

3 Neutral

2 Disagree

1 Strongly Disagree

1. Are the Service Applications requirements complete?
<--- Score

2. When is/was the Service Applications start date?
<--- Score

3. Are improvement team members fully trained on Service Applications?

<--- Score

4. What are the rough order estimates on cost savings/ opportunities that Service Applications brings?
<--- Score

5. Are there different segments of customers?
<--- Score

6. Does the scope remain the same?
<--- Score

7. How do you gather requirements?
<--- Score

8. What is in scope?
<--- Score

9. What are the dynamics of the communication plan?
<--- Score

10. Will team members perform Service Applications work when assigned and in a timely fashion?
<--- Score

11. How do you keep key subject matter experts in the loop?
<--- Score

12. What are the Service Applications use cases?
<--- Score

13. What Service Applications services do you require?
<--- Score

14. How do you manage unclear Service Applications

requirements?
<--- Score

15. How was the 'as is' process map developed, reviewed, verified and validated?
<--- Score

16. Is scope creep really all bad news?
<--- Score

17. Are required metrics defined, what are they?
<--- Score

18. What is the scope of Service Applications?
<--- Score

19. What gets examined?
<--- Score

20. How will variation in the actual durations of each activity be dealt with to ensure that the expected Service Applications results are met?
<--- Score

21. Where can you gather more information?
<--- Score

22. Is it clearly defined in and to your organization what you do?
<--- Score

23. What specifically is the problem? Where does it occur? When does it occur? What is its extent?
<--- Score

24. Who defines (or who defined) the rules and roles?

<--- Score

25. How do you gather Service Applications requirements?
<--- Score

26. How would you define Service Applications leadership?
<--- Score

27. What knowledge or experience is required?
<--- Score

28. Do you have organizational privacy requirements?
<--- Score

29. What information should you gather?
<--- Score

30. Are accountability and ownership for Service Applications clearly defined?
<--- Score

31. If substitutes have been appointed, have they been briefed on the Service Applications goals and received regular communications as to the progress to date?
<--- Score

32. How do you think the partners involved in Service Applications would have defined success?
<--- Score

33. Will a Service Applications production readiness review be required?
<--- Score

34. Who is gathering information?
<--- Score

35. What was the context?
<--- Score

36. How did the Service Applications manager receive input to the development of a Service Applications improvement plan and the estimated completion dates/times of each activity?
<--- Score

37. Are customer(s) identified and segmented according to their different needs and requirements?
<--- Score

38. Is special Service Applications user knowledge required?
<--- Score

39. When is the estimated completion date?
<--- Score

40. What scope to assess?
<--- Score

41. What are (control) requirements for Service Applications Information?
<--- Score

42. Is the Service Applications scope complete and appropriately sized?
<--- Score

43. Who are the Service Applications improvement

team members, including Management Leads and Coaches?

<--- Score

44. Is there a clear Service Applications case definition?

<--- Score

45. What is out-of-scope initially?

<--- Score

46. Are the Service Applications requirements testable?

<--- Score

47. What is the scope of the Service Applications effort?

<--- Score

48. What scope do you want your strategy to cover?

<--- Score

49. Do you have a Service Applications success story or case study ready to tell and share?

<--- Score

50. How have you defined all Service Applications requirements first?

<--- Score

51. Has a team charter been developed and communicated?

<--- Score

52. What defines best in class?

<--- Score

53. In what way can you redefine the criteria of choice clients have in your category in your favor?

<--- Score

54. Is Service Applications currently on schedule according to the plan?

<--- Score

55. What is in the scope and what is not in scope?

<--- Score

56. What are the tasks and definitions?

<--- Score

57. What would be the goal or target for a Service Applications's improvement team?

<--- Score

58. Is Service Applications required?

<--- Score

59. Is there a critical path to deliver Service Applications results?

<--- Score

60. Is full participation by members in regularly held team meetings guaranteed?

<--- Score

61. The political context: who holds power?

<--- Score

62. How do you catch Service Applications definition inconsistencies?

<--- Score

63. What key stakeholder process output measure(s) does Service Applications leverage and how?
<--- Score

64. What is the definition of success?
<--- Score

65. What information do you gather?
<--- Score

66. Has the improvement team collected the 'voice of the customer' (obtained feedback – qualitative and quantitative)?
<--- Score

67. Are resources adequate for the scope?
<--- Score

68. Is data collected and displayed to better understand customer(s) critical needs and requirements.
<--- Score

69. Who approved the Service Applications scope?
<--- Score

70. When are meeting minutes sent out? Who is on the distribution list?
<--- Score

71. Has the direction changed at all during the course of Service Applications? If so, when did it change and why?
<--- Score

72. What intelligence can you gather?
<--- Score

73. Has a high-level 'as is' process map been completed, verified and validated?
<--- Score

74. Scope of sensitive information?
<--- Score

75. How is the team tracking and documenting its work?
<--- Score

76. What happens if Service Applications's scope changes?
<--- Score

77. Has/have the customer(s) been identified?
<--- Score

78. Is Service Applications linked to key stakeholder goals and objectives?
<--- Score

79. Are task requirements clearly defined?
<--- Score

80. How do you hand over Service Applications context?
<--- Score

81. How do you manage scope?
<--- Score

82. What baselines are required to be defined and

managed?

<--- Score

83. Is the current 'as is' process being followed? If not, what are the discrepancies?

<--- Score

84. Is there a completed SIPOC representation, describing the Suppliers, Inputs, Process, Outputs, and Customers?

<--- Score

85. Have all basic functions of Service Applications been defined?

<--- Score

86. How would you define the culture at your organization, how susceptible is it to Service Applications changes?

<--- Score

87. Has a project plan, Gantt chart, or similar been developed/completed?

<--- Score

88. How does the Service Applications manager ensure against scope creep?

<--- Score

89. Do you all define Service Applications in the same way?

<--- Score

90. How and when will the baselines be defined?

<--- Score

91. How will the Service Applications team and the group measure complete success of Service Applications?
<--- Score

92. Who is gathering Service Applications information?
<--- Score

93. Is there a completed, verified, and validated high-level 'as is' (not 'should be' or 'could be') stakeholder process map?
<--- Score

94. Has your scope been defined?
<--- Score

95. Are roles and responsibilities formally defined?
<--- Score

96. Is the Service Applications scope manageable?
<--- Score

97. What are the Roles and Responsibilities for each team member and its leadership? Where is this documented?
<--- Score

98. What is the worst case scenario?
<--- Score

99. How do you build the right business case?
<--- Score

100. Is the team adequately staffed with the desired cross-functionality? If not, what additional resources

are available to the team?
<--- Score

101. Has a Service Applications requirement not been met?
<--- Score

102. Is the team equipped with available and reliable resources?
<--- Score

103. What Service Applications requirements should be gathered?
<--- Score

104. What are the compelling stakeholder reasons for embarking on Service Applications?
<--- Score

105. Has everyone on the team, including the team leaders, been properly trained?
<--- Score

106. What customer feedback methods were used to solicit their input?
<--- Score

107. How do you manage changes in Service Applications requirements?
<--- Score

108. What constraints exist that might impact the team?
<--- Score

109. Are there any constraints known that bear on the

ability to perform Service Applications work? How is the team addressing them?

<--- Score

110. Are approval levels defined for contracts and supplements to contracts?

<--- Score

111. Is the improvement team aware of the different versions of a process: what they think it is vs. what it actually is vs. what it should be vs. what it could be?

<--- Score

112. What critical content must be communicated – who, what, when, where, and how?

<--- Score

113. Is the work to date meeting requirements?

<--- Score

114. Do the problem and goal statements meet the SMART criteria (specific, measurable, attainable, relevant, and time-bound)?

<--- Score

115. How do you gather the stories?

<--- Score

116. What is the scope?

<--- Score

117. What sources do you use to gather information for a Service Applications study?

<--- Score

118. Is there regularly 100% attendance at the

team meetings? If not, have appointed substitutes attended to preserve cross-functionality and full representation?

<--- Score

119. What is the scope of the Service Applications work?

<--- Score

120. Are audit criteria, scope, frequency and methods defined?

<--- Score

121. How often are the team meetings?

<--- Score

122. What are the core elements of the Service Applications business case?

<--- Score

123. Does the team have regular meetings?

<--- Score

124. What system do you use for gathering Service Applications information?

<--- Score

125. Have the customer needs been translated into specific, measurable requirements? How?

<--- Score

126. What are the requirements for audit information?

<--- Score

127. What are the record-keeping requirements of Service Applications activities?

<--- Score

128. What is a worst-case scenario for losses?
<--- Score

129. Will team members regularly document their Service Applications work?
<--- Score

130. What is the context?
<--- Score

131. How are consistent Service Applications definitions important?
<--- Score

132. Has the Service Applications work been fairly and/or equitably divided and delegated among team members who are qualified and capable to perform the work? Has everyone contributed?
<--- Score

133. Is there a Service Applications management charter, including stakeholder case, problem and goal statements, scope, milestones, roles and responsibilities, communication plan?
<--- Score

134. Is there any additional Service Applications definition of success?
<--- Score

135. Has anyone else (internal or external to the group) attempted to solve this problem or a similar one before? If so, what knowledge can be leveraged from these previous efforts?

<--- Score

136. Have specific policy objectives been defined?
<--- Score

137. Is the scope of Service Applications defined?
<--- Score

138. What are the Service Applications tasks and definitions?
<--- Score

139. Are different versions of process maps needed to account for the different types of inputs?
<--- Score

140. What are the boundaries of the scope? What is in bounds and what is not? What is the start point? What is the stop point?
<--- Score

Add up total points for this section:
_____ = Total points for this section

Divided by: _____ (number of statements answered) = _____
Average score for this section

Transfer your score to the Service Applications Index at the beginning of the Self-Assessment.

CRITERION #3: MEASURE:

INTENT: Gather the correct data.
Measure the current performance and
evolution of the situation.

In my belief, the answer to this
question is clearly defined:

5 Strongly Agree

4 Agree

3 Neutral

2 Disagree

1 Strongly Disagree

1. What are the Service Applications investment costs?
<--- Score

2. Why do the measurements/indicators matter?
<--- Score

3. Is the cost worth the Service Applications effort ?
<--- Score

4. Does management have the right priorities among projects?
<--- Score

5. What is the total fixed cost?
<--- Score

6. Are there any easy-to-implement alternatives to Service Applications? Sometimes other solutions are available that do not require the cost implications of a full-blown project?
<--- Score

7. What can be used to verify compliance?
<--- Score

8. How will you measure success?
<--- Score

9. How are costs allocated?
<--- Score

10. Who is involved in verifying compliance?
<--- Score

11. What are the operational costs after Service Applications deployment?
<--- Score

12. How do you verify the authenticity of the data and information used?
<--- Score

13. What causes extra work or rework?
<--- Score

14. How long to keep data and how to manage retention costs?
<--- Score

15. Is it possible to estimate the impact of unanticipated complexity such as wrong or failed assumptions, feedback, etcetera on proposed reforms?
<--- Score

16. How much does it cost?
<--- Score

17. What would be a real cause for concern?
<--- Score

18. Do you have an issue in getting priority?
<--- Score

19. Are Service Applications vulnerabilities categorized and prioritized?
<--- Score

20. Are the units of measure consistent?
<--- Score

21. How frequently do you verify your Service Applications strategy?
<--- Score

22. How can you measure Service Applications in a systematic way?
<--- Score

23. The approach of traditional Service Applications works for detail complexity but is focused on a

systematic approach rather than an understanding of the nature of systems themselves, what approach will permit your organization to deal with the kind of unpredictable emergent behaviors that dynamic complexity can introduce?

<--- Score

24. How do you quantify and qualify impacts?

<--- Score

25. What details are required of the Service Applications cost structure?

<--- Score

26. What are your customers expectations and measures?

<--- Score

27. What are your key Service Applications organizational performance measures, including key short and longer-term financial measures?

<--- Score

28. How are you verifying it?

<--- Score

29. What is the cause of any Service Applications gaps?

<--- Score

30. How can you reduce costs?

<--- Score

31. How will success or failure be measured?

<--- Score

32. What are the Service Applications key cost drivers?
<--- Score

33. Are the Service Applications benefits worth its costs?
<--- Score

34. Have you included everything in your Service Applications cost models?
<--- Score

35. Have you made assumptions about the shape of the future, particularly its impact on your customers and competitors?
<--- Score

36. Among the Service Applications product and service cost to be estimated, which is considered hardest to estimate?
<--- Score

37. Do you aggressively reward and promote the people who have the biggest impact on creating excellent Service Applications services/products?
<--- Score

38. How will measures be used to manage and adapt?
<--- Score

39. Why a Service Applications focus?
<--- Score

40. Has a cost center been established?
<--- Score

41. What methods are feasible and acceptable to

estimate the impact of reforms?
<--- Score

42. What does your operating model cost?
<--- Score

43. Are indirect costs charged to the Service
Applications program?
<--- Score

44. At what cost?
<--- Score

45. How do you measure success?
<--- Score

46. How do you aggregate measures across priorities?
<--- Score

47. Where can you go to verify the info?
<--- Score

48. Are actual costs in line with budgeted costs?
<--- Score

49. Does a Service Applications quantification method
exist?
<--- Score

50. What tests verify requirements?
<--- Score

51. What are the estimated costs of proposed
changes?
<--- Score

52. How do you verify if Service Applications is built right?

<--- Score

53. How will costs be allocated?

<--- Score

54. What is your Service Applications quality cost segregation study?

<--- Score

55. Are you taking your company in the direction of better and revenue or cheaper and cost?

<--- Score

56. How do you focus on what is right -not who is right?

<--- Score

57. What is the Service Applications business impact?

<--- Score

58. Where is it measured?

<--- Score

59. What are allowable costs?

<--- Score

60. Which measures and indicators matter?

<--- Score

61. Do you have a flow diagram of what happens?

<--- Score

62. Are you able to realize any cost savings?

<--- Score

63. What does a Test Case verify?
<--- Score

64. How is progress measured?
<--- Score

65. Do you verify that corrective actions were taken?
<--- Score

66. How do you control the overall costs of your work processes?
<--- Score

67. How can you manage cost down?
<--- Score

68. When a disaster occurs, who gets priority?
<--- Score

69. What are you verifying?
<--- Score

70. What do you measure and why?
<--- Score

71. How to cause the change?
<--- Score

72. Are supply costs steady or fluctuating?
<--- Score

73. How frequently do you track Service Applications measures?
<--- Score

74. How do you verify and validate the Service Applications data?
<--- Score

75. How can you reduce the costs of obtaining inputs?
<--- Score

76. What harm might be caused?
<--- Score

77. How do you measure efficient delivery of Service Applications services?
<--- Score

78. What are the uncertainties surrounding estimates of impact?
<--- Score

79. What would it cost to replace your technology?
<--- Score

80. Which costs should be taken into account?
<--- Score

81. How sensitive must the Service Applications strategy be to cost?
<--- Score

82. What could cause delays in the schedule?
<--- Score

83. What are the types and number of measures to use?
<--- Score

84. Who pays the cost?

<--- Score

85. How do you verify the Service Applications requirements quality?
<--- Score

86. How are measurements made?
<--- Score

87. Do you have any cost Service Applications limitation requirements?
<--- Score

88. How can a Service Applications test verify your ideas or assumptions?
<--- Score

89. How can you measure the performance?
<--- Score

90. How do you measure variability?
<--- Score

91. What are your primary costs, revenues, assets?
<--- Score

92. What are the costs?
<--- Score

93. Have design-to-cost goals been established?
<--- Score

94. What evidence is there and what is measured?
<--- Score

95. What is your decision requirements diagram?

<--- Score

96. What are your operating costs?
<--- Score

97. How do you verify and develop ideas and innovations?
<--- Score

98. Do the benefits outweigh the costs?
<--- Score

99. Who should receive measurement reports?
<--- Score

100. How is performance measured?
<--- Score

101. Is there an opportunity to verify requirements?
<--- Score

102. Was a business case (cost/benefit) developed?
<--- Score

103. When are costs are incurred?
<--- Score

104. How do you measure lifecycle phases?
<--- Score

105. Are the measurements objective?
<--- Score

106. What disadvantage does this cause for the user?
<--- Score

107. What relevant entities could be measured?
<--- Score

108. What are the costs and benefits?
<--- Score

109. What is the root cause(s) of the problem?
<--- Score

110. Are there measurements based on task performance?
<--- Score

111. Did you tackle the cause or the symptom?
<--- Score

112. Do you effectively measure and reward individual and team performance?
<--- Score

113. What potential environmental factors impact the Service Applications effort?
<--- Score

114. How will you measure your Service Applications effectiveness?
<--- Score

115. Is the solution cost-effective?
<--- Score

116. What are the costs of reform?
<--- Score

117. How do you prevent mis-estimating cost?
<--- Score

118. What is measured? Why?
<--- Score

119. Are you aware of what could cause a problem?
<--- Score

120. What causes investor action?
<--- Score

121. What measurements are possible, practicable and meaningful?
<--- Score

122. What users will be impacted?
<--- Score

123. What are hidden Service Applications quality costs?
<--- Score

124. How do your measurements capture actionable Service Applications information for use in exceeding your customers expectations and securing your customers engagement?
<--- Score

125. What happens if cost savings do not materialize?
<--- Score

126. What causes mismanagement?
<--- Score

127. Does the Service Applications task fit the client's priorities?
<--- Score

128. How do you verify Service Applications completeness and accuracy?
<--- Score

129. Why do you expend time and effort to implement measurement, for whom?
<--- Score

130. How do you verify your resources?
<--- Score

131. What are the current costs of the Service Applications process?
<--- Score

132. What could cause you to change course?
<--- Score

133. Will Service Applications have an impact on current business continuity, disaster recovery processes and/or infrastructure?
<--- Score

134. Where is the cost?
<--- Score

135. Which Service Applications impacts are significant?
<--- Score

136. How do you stay flexible and focused to recognize larger Service Applications results?
<--- Score

137. When should you bother with diagrams?

<--- Score

138. Are missed Service Applications opportunities costing your organization money?
<--- Score

139. How will effects be measured?
<--- Score

140. How do you verify performance?
<--- Score

141. How is the value delivered by Service Applications being measured?
<--- Score

142. What causes innovation to fail or succeed in your organization?
<--- Score

Add up total points for this section:
_ _ _ _ _ = Total points for this section

Divided by: _ _ _ _ _ _ (number of statements answered) = _ _ _ _ _ _
Average score for this section

Transfer your score to the Service Applications Index at the beginning of the Self-Assessment.

CRITERION #4: ANALYZE:

INTENT: Analyze causes, assumptions and hypotheses.

In my belief, the answer to this question is clearly defined:

5 Strongly Agree

4 Agree

3 Neutral

2 Disagree

1 Strongly Disagree

1. Is there an established change management process?
<--- Score

2. Are your outputs consistent?
<--- Score

3. What tools were used to narrow the list of possible causes?
<--- Score

4. How will the change process be managed?
<--- Score

5. Who owns what data?
<--- Score

6. How is data used for program management and improvement?
<--- Score

7. Can you add value to the current Service Applications decision-making process (largely qualitative) by incorporating uncertainty modeling (more quantitative)?
<--- Score

8. Do you have the authority to produce the output?
<--- Score

9. Is data and process analysis, root cause analysis and quantifying the gap/opportunity in place?
<--- Score

10. What qualifications and skills do you need?
<--- Score

11. How do you identify specific Service Applications investment opportunities and emerging trends?
<--- Score

12. Identify an operational issue in your organization, for example, could a particular task be done more quickly or more efficiently by Service Applications?
<--- Score

13. Did any additional data need to be collected?
<--- Score

14. Are you missing Service Applications opportunities?
<--- Score

15. Were Pareto charts (or similar) used to portray the 'heavy hitters' (or key sources of variation)?
<--- Score

16. What other organizational variables, such as reward systems or communication systems, affect the performance of this Service Applications process?
<--- Score

17. What do you need to qualify?
<--- Score

18. Is the performance gap determined?
<--- Score

19. How are outputs preserved and protected?
<--- Score

20. Who will gather what data?
<--- Score

21. Was a detailed process map created to amplify critical steps of the 'as is' stakeholder process?
<--- Score

22. What is the Service Applications Driver?
<--- Score

23. Where is the data coming from to measure

compliance?
<--- Score

24. Record-keeping requirements flow from the records needed as inputs, outputs, controls and for transformation of a Service Applications process, are the records needed as inputs to the Service Applications process available?
<--- Score

25. Where can you get qualified talent today?
<--- Score

26. What are the best opportunities for value improvement?
<--- Score

27. Has an output goal been set?
<--- Score

28. What is the Value Stream Mapping?
<--- Score

29. What internal processes need improvement?
<--- Score

30. How do you ensure that the Service Applications opportunity is realistic?
<--- Score

31. What were the crucial 'moments of truth' on the process map?
<--- Score

32. What other jobs or tasks affect the performance of the steps in the Service Applications process?

<--- Score

33. Who gets your output?
<--- Score

34. An organizationally feasible system request is one that considers the mission, goals and objectives of the organization, key questions are: is the Service Applications solution request practical and will it solve a problem or take advantage of an opportunity to achieve company goals?
<--- Score

35. Were there any improvement opportunities identified from the process analysis?
<--- Score

36. How will the Service Applications data be captured?
<--- Score

37. What methods do you use to gather Service Applications data?
<--- Score

38. Was a cause-and-effect diagram used to explore the different types of causes (or sources of variation)?
<--- Score

39. What quality tools were used to get through the analyze phase?
<--- Score

40. What process should you select for improvement?
<--- Score

41. What are the personnel training and qualifications required?

<--- Score

42. How is the Service Applications Value Stream Mapping managed?

<--- Score

43. What are the necessary qualifications?

<--- Score

44. How do your work systems and key work processes relate to and capitalize on your core competencies?

<--- Score

45. Do you understand your management processes today?

<--- Score

46. What Service Applications data should be collected?

<--- Score

47. What qualifications do Service Applications leaders need?

<--- Score

48. Which Service Applications data should be retained?

<--- Score

49. What qualifications are necessary?

<--- Score

50. What Service Applications data will be collected?

<--- Score

51. What were the financial benefits resulting from any 'ground fruit or low-hanging fruit' (quick fixes)?
<--- Score

52. Have any additional benefits been identified that will result from closing all or most of the gaps?
<--- Score

53. Has data output been validated?
<--- Score

54. How can risk management be tied procedurally to process elements?
<--- Score

55. Do you, as a leader, bounce back quickly from setbacks?
<--- Score

56. When should a process be art not science?
<--- Score

57. Is pre-qualification of suppliers carried out?
<--- Score

58. What data is gathered?
<--- Score

59. What will drive Service Applications change?
<--- Score

60. What are the processes for audit reporting and management?
<--- Score

61. Did any value-added analysis or 'lean thinking' take place to identify some of the gaps shown on the 'as is' process map?
<--- Score

62. What data do you need to collect?
<--- Score

63. Who will facilitate the team and process?
<--- Score

64. How do you measure the operational performance of your key work systems and processes, including productivity, cycle time, and other appropriate measures of process effectiveness, efficiency, and innovation?
<--- Score

65. Is the suppliers process defined and controlled?
<--- Score

66. What did the team gain from developing a sub-process map?
<--- Score

67. What does the data say about the performance of the stakeholder process?
<--- Score

68. Are all team members qualified for all tasks?
<--- Score

69. What qualifications are needed?
<--- Score

70. What process improvements will be needed?
<--- Score

71. Do staff qualifications match your project?
<--- Score

72. How does the organization define, manage, and improve its Service Applications processes?
<--- Score

73. What output to create?
<--- Score

74. Do your employees have the opportunity to do what they do best everyday?
<--- Score

75. How many input/output points does it require?
<--- Score

76. Where is Service Applications data gathered?
<--- Score

77. How is Service Applications data gathered?
<--- Score

78. Were any designed experiments used to generate additional insight into the data analysis?
<--- Score

79. What types of data do your Service Applications indicators require?
<--- Score

80. What training and qualifications will you need?
<--- Score

81. What information qualified as important?
<--- Score

82. What is your organizations system for selecting qualified vendors?
<--- Score

83. What conclusions were drawn from the team's data collection and analysis? How did the team reach these conclusions?
<--- Score

84. What resources go in to get the desired output?
<--- Score

85. How is the way you as the leader think and process information affecting your organizational culture?
<--- Score

86. Is the required Service Applications data gathered?
<--- Score

87. What are the disruptive Service Applications technologies that enable your organization to radically change your business processes?
<--- Score

88. How do you promote understanding that opportunity for improvement is not criticism of the status quo, or the people who created the status quo?
<--- Score

89. How is the data gathered?
<--- Score

90. What kind of crime could a potential new hire have committed that would not only not disqualify him/her from being hired by your organization, but would actually indicate that he/she might be a particularly good fit?
<--- Score

91. Do your contracts/agreements contain data security obligations?
<--- Score

92. Do several people in different organizational units assist with the Service Applications process?
<--- Score

93. How difficult is it to qualify what Service Applications ROI is?
<--- Score

94. Is there any way to speed up the process?
<--- Score

95. How has the Service Applications data been gathered?
<--- Score

96. What, related to, Service Applications processes does your organization outsource?
<--- Score

97. How often will data be collected for measures?
<--- Score

98. Who is involved in the management review process?

<--- Score

99. Are all staff in core Service Applications subjects Highly Qualified?
<--- Score

100. What systems/processes must you excel at?
<--- Score

101. Think about some of the processes you undertake within your organization, which do you own?
<--- Score

102. What are your current levels and trends in key measures or indicators of Service Applications product and process performance that are important to and directly serve your customers? How do these results compare with the performance of your competitors and other organizations with similar offerings?
<--- Score

103. What are the revised rough estimates of the financial savings/opportunity for Service Applications improvements?
<--- Score

104. Is the final output clearly identified?
<--- Score

105. How do you define collaboration and team output?
<--- Score

106. Have you defined which data is gathered how?

<--- Score

107. What is the cost of poor quality as supported by the team's analysis?
<--- Score

108. What are the Service Applications design outputs?
<--- Score

109. How much data can be collected in the given timeframe?
<--- Score

110. What is the oversight process?
<--- Score

111. What are the Service Applications business drivers?
<--- Score

112. Who is involved with workflow mapping?
<--- Score

113. What Service Applications metrics are outputs of the process?
<--- Score

114. What is the complexity of the output produced?
<--- Score

115. How will corresponding data be collected?
<--- Score

116. What are evaluation criteria for the output?
<--- Score

117. How was the detailed process map generated, verified, and validated?
<--- Score

118. What tools were used to generate the list of possible causes?
<--- Score

119. How do you implement and manage your work processes to ensure that they meet design requirements?
<--- Score

120. What Service Applications data should be managed?
<--- Score

121. Is the Service Applications process severely broken such that a re-design is necessary?
<--- Score

122. Do your leaders quickly bounce back from setbacks?
<--- Score

123. What qualifies as competition?
<--- Score

124. Think about the functions involved in your Service Applications project, what processes flow from these functions?
<--- Score

125. Do quality systems drive continuous improvement?

<--- Score

126. How will the data be checked for quality?
<--- Score

127. What is your organizations process which leads
to recognition of value generation?
<--- Score

128. What controls do you have in place to protect
data?
<--- Score

129. A compounding model resolution with available
relevant data can often provide insight towards a
solution methodology; which Service Applications
models, tools and techniques are necessary?
<--- Score

130. Have the problem and goal statements been
updated to reflect the additional knowledge gained
from the analyze phase?
<--- Score

131. Who qualifies to gain access to data?
<--- Score

132. What is the output?
<--- Score

133. Is there a strict change management process?
<--- Score

134. Is the gap/opportunity displayed and
communicated in financial terms?
<--- Score

Add up total points for this section:
_ _ _ _ _ = Total points for this section

Divided by: _ _ _ _ _ _ (number of
statements answered) = _ _ _ _ _ _
Average score for this section

Transfer your score to the Service
Applications Index at the beginning of
the Self-Assessment.

CRITERION #5: IMPROVE:

INTENT: Develop a practical solution. Innovate, establish and test the solution and to measure the results.

In my belief, the answer to this question is clearly defined:

5 Strongly Agree

4 Agree

3 Neutral

2 Disagree

1 Strongly Disagree

1. Risk Identification: What are the possible risk events your organization faces in relation to Service Applications?
<--- Score

2. What error proofing will be done to address some of the discrepancies observed in the 'as is' process?
<--- Score

3. What criteria will you use to assess your Service Applications risks?
<--- Score

4. Are risk triggers captured?
<--- Score

5. How do the Service Applications results compare with the performance of your competitors and other organizations with similar offerings?
<--- Score

6. What actually has to improve and by how much?
<--- Score

7. Who are the key stakeholders for the Service Applications evaluation?
<--- Score

8. Is the scope clearly documented?
<--- Score

9. Does a good decision guarantee a good outcome?
<--- Score

10. What are the Service Applications security risks?
<--- Score

11. What should a proof of concept or pilot accomplish?
<--- Score

12. How do you manage and improve your Service Applications work systems to deliver customer value and achieve organizational success and sustainability?
<--- Score

13. When you map the key players in your own work and the types/domains of relationships with them, which relationships do you find easy and which challenging, and why?
<--- Score

14. How do you improve your likelihood of success ?
<--- Score

15. How will you know that a change is an improvement?
<--- Score

16. How can the phases of Service Applications development be identified?
<--- Score

17. How do you measure progress and evaluate training effectiveness?
<--- Score

18. How significant is the improvement in the eyes of the end user?
<--- Score

19. Who should make the Service Applications decisions?
<--- Score

20. What are the concrete Service Applications results?
<--- Score

21. What were the underlying assumptions on the cost-benefit analysis?

<--- Score

22. How do you link measurement and risk?
<--- Score

23. Risk events: what are the things that could go wrong?
<--- Score

24. Is there any other Service Applications solution?
<--- Score

25. How do you deal with Service Applications risk?
<--- Score

26. What are the affordable Service Applications risks?
<--- Score

27. Explorations of the frontiers of Service Applications will help you build influence, improve Service Applications, optimize decision making, and sustain change, what is your approach?
<--- Score

28. Can the solution be designed and implemented within an acceptable time period?
<--- Score

29. How do you measure improved Service Applications service perception, and satisfaction?
<--- Score

30. Who controls the risk?
<--- Score

31. Would you develop a Service Applications

Communication Strategy?
<--- Score

32. Do you have the optimal project management team structure?
<--- Score

33. Are the risks fully understood, reasonable and manageable?
<--- Score

34. Are the key business and technology risks being managed?
<--- Score

35. How do you decide how much to remunerate an employee?
<--- Score

36. Is there a high likelihood that any recommendations will achieve their intended results?
<--- Score

37. Do you need to do a usability evaluation?
<--- Score

38. What is the risk?
<--- Score

39. How will you know that you have improved?
<--- Score

40. Can you integrate quality management and risk management?
<--- Score

41. Who manages Service Applications risk?
<--- Score

42. How are policy decisions made and where?
<--- Score

43. Are decisions made in a timely manner?
<--- Score

44. What to do with the results or outcomes of measurements?
<--- Score

45. For estimation problems, how do you develop an estimation statement?
<--- Score

46. Who manages supplier risk management in your organization?
<--- Score

47. For decision problems, how do you develop a decision statement?
<--- Score

48. How do you keep improving Service Applications?
<--- Score

49. How do you define the solutions' scope?
<--- Score

50. How does the team improve its work?
<--- Score

51. Are you assessing Service Applications and risk?
<--- Score

52. How will you know when its improved?
<--- Score

53. How do you improve productivity?
<--- Score

54. What is the implementation plan?
<--- Score

55. What resources are required for the improvement efforts?
<--- Score

56. What lessons, if any, from a pilot were incorporated into the design of the full-scale solution?
<--- Score

57. How is knowledge sharing about risk management improved?
<--- Score

58. What practices helps your organization to develop its capacity to recognize patterns?
<--- Score

59. In the past few months, what is the smallest change you have made that has had the biggest positive result? What was it about that small change that produced the large return?
<--- Score

60. Does the goal represent a desired result that can be measured?
<--- Score

61. What current systems have to be understood and/ or changed?
<--- Score

62. Have you achieved Service Applications improvements?
<--- Score

63. How scalable is your Service Applications solution?
<--- Score

64. Risk factors: what are the characteristics of Service Applications that make it risky?
<--- Score

65. What are the implications of the one critical Service Applications decision 10 minutes, 10 months, and 10 years from now?
<--- Score

66. Will the controls trigger any other risks?
<--- Score

67. What area needs the greatest improvement?
<--- Score

68. What are the expected Service Applications results?
<--- Score

69. What tools were used to evaluate the potential solutions?
<--- Score

70. How do you improve Service Applications service perception, and satisfaction?

<--- Score

71. Who makes the Service Applications decisions in your organization?
<--- Score

72. What improvements have been achieved?
<--- Score

73. Is the solution technically practical?
<--- Score

74. What is the team's contingency plan for potential problems occurring in implementation?
<--- Score

75. What tools were most useful during the improve phase?
<--- Score

76. What tools do you use once you have decided on a Service Applications strategy and more importantly how do you choose?
<--- Score

77. Is the Service Applications solution sustainable?
<--- Score

78. What assumptions are made about the solution and approach?
<--- Score

79. Service Applications risk decisions: whose call Is It?
<--- Score

80. Who will be responsible for making the decisions

to include or exclude requested changes once Service Applications is underway?
<--- Score

81. Where do you need Service Applications improvement?
<--- Score

82. Have you identified breakpoints and/or risk tolerances that will trigger broad consideration of a potential need for intervention or modification of strategy?
<--- Score

83. Who are the Service Applications decision makers?
<--- Score

84. How are Service Applications risks managed?
<--- Score

85. What is the Service Applications's sustainability risk?
<--- Score

86. What needs improvement? Why?
<--- Score

87. Is any Service Applications documentation required?
<--- Score

88. Who controls key decisions that will be made?
<--- Score

89. How will you recognize and celebrate results?
<--- Score

90. Who are the Service Applications decision-makers?
<--- Score

91. How can skill-level changes improve Service Applications?
<--- Score

92. How does your organization evaluate strategic Service Applications success?
<--- Score

93. What alternative responses are available to manage risk?
<--- Score

94. What Service Applications improvements can be made?
<--- Score

95. What went well, what should change, what can improve?
<--- Score

96. Do you cover the five essential competencies: Communication, Collaboration,Innovation, Adaptability, and Leadership that improve an organizations ability to leverage the new Service Applications in a volatile global economy?
<--- Score

97. What communications are necessary to support the implementation of the solution?
<--- Score

98. What can you do to improve?

<--- Score

99. How risky is your organization?
<--- Score

100. What do you want to improve?
<--- Score

101. Is the Service Applications risk managed?
<--- Score

102. Do you combine technical expertise with business knowledge and Service Applications Key topics include lifecycles, development approaches, requirements and how to make a business case?
<--- Score

103. Are risk management tasks balanced centrally and locally?
<--- Score

104. Are the most efficient solutions problem-specific?
<--- Score

105. What is the magnitude of the improvements?
<--- Score

106. Can you identify any significant risks or exposures to Service Applications third- parties (vendors, service providers, alliance partners etc) that concern you?
<--- Score

107. Is the Service Applications documentation thorough?
<--- Score

108. What is Service Applications risk?
<--- Score

109. How do you mitigate Service Applications risk?
<--- Score

110. Who are the people involved in developing and implementing Service Applications?
<--- Score

111. What were the criteria for evaluating a Service Applications pilot?
<--- Score

112. How can you improve performance?
<--- Score

113. Do those selected for the Service Applications team have a good general understanding of what Service Applications is all about?
<--- Score

114. How can you better manage risk?
<--- Score

115. Are procedures documented for managing Service Applications risks?
<--- Score

116. Is risk periodically assessed?
<--- Score

117. Is Service Applications documentation maintained?
<--- Score

118. At what point will vulnerability assessments be performed once Service Applications is put into production (e.g., ongoing Risk Management after implementation)?
<--- Score

119. How do you manage Service Applications risk?
<--- Score

120. What tools were used to tap into the creativity and encourage 'outside the box' thinking?
<--- Score

121. Where do the Service Applications decisions reside?
<--- Score

122. Do vendor agreements bring new compliance risk ?
<--- Score

123. Who will be using the results of the measurement activities?
<--- Score

124. To what extent does management recognize Service Applications as a tool to increase the results?
<--- Score

125. Are events managed to resolution?
<--- Score

126. What strategies for Service Applications improvement are successful?
<--- Score

127. What is Service Applications's impact on utilizing the best solution(s)?
<--- Score

128. What does the 'should be' process map/design look like?
<--- Score

129. What are your current levels and trends in key measures or indicators of workforce and leader development?
<--- Score

130. What risks do you need to manage?
<--- Score

131. How do you go about comparing Service Applications approaches/solutions?
<--- Score

132. How can you improve Service Applications?
<--- Score

133. Who do you report Service Applications results to?
<--- Score

134. Is the measure of success for Service Applications understandable to a variety of people?
<--- Score

135. Was a Service Applications charter developed?
<--- Score

136. Why improve in the first place?
<--- Score

137. How is continuous improvement applied to risk management?
<--- Score

Add up total points for this section:
_____ = Total points for this section

Divided by: _____ (number of
statements answered) = _____
Average score for this section

Transfer your score to the Service
Applications Index at the beginning of
the Self-Assessment.

CRITERION #6: CONTROL:

INTENT: Implement the practical solution. Maintain the performance and correct possible complications.

In my belief, the answer to this question is clearly defined:

5 Strongly Agree

4 Agree

3 Neutral

2 Disagree

1 Strongly Disagree

1. How widespread is its use?
<--- Score

2. Is the Service Applications test/monitoring cost justified?
<--- Score

3. What other systems, operations, processes, and infrastructures (hiring practices, staffing, training,

incentives/rewards, metrics/dashboards/scorecards, etc.) need updates, additions, changes, or deletions in order to facilitate knowledge transfer and improvements?
<--- Score

4. What should the next improvement project be that is related to Service Applications?
<--- Score

5. Who has control over resources?
<--- Score

6. How will input, process, and output variables be checked to detect for sub-optimal conditions?
<--- Score

7. How is Service Applications project cost planned, managed, monitored?
<--- Score

8. Does the Service Applications performance meet the customer's requirements?
<--- Score

9. How do senior leaders actions reflect a commitment to the organizations Service Applications values?
<--- Score

10. How likely is the current Service Applications plan to come in on schedule or on budget?
<--- Score

11. Is a response plan in place for when the input, process, or output measures indicate an 'out-of-

control' condition?

<--- Score

12. How might the group capture best practices and lessons learned so as to leverage improvements?

<--- Score

13. What are customers monitoring?

<--- Score

14. Act/Adjust: What Do you Need to Do Differently?

<--- Score

15. What other areas of the group might benefit from the Service Applications team's improvements, knowledge, and learning?

<--- Score

16. Does the response plan contain a definite closed loop continual improvement scheme (e.g., plan-do-check-act)?

<--- Score

17. Can support from partners be adjusted?

<--- Score

18. Do you monitor the Service Applications decisions made and fine tune them as they evolve?

<--- Score

19. What is your theory of human motivation, and how does your compensation plan fit with that view?

<--- Score

20. How will you measure your QA plan's effectiveness?

<--- Score

21. Will existing staff require re-training, for example, to learn new business processes?
<--- Score

22. Are operating procedures consistent?
<--- Score

23. What can you control?
<--- Score

24. How do you spread information?
<--- Score

25. How will report readings be checked to effectively monitor performance?
<--- Score

26. Does a troubleshooting guide exist or is it needed?
<--- Score

27. Is there a standardized process?
<--- Score

28. What are your results for key measures or indicators of the accomplishment of your Service Applications strategy and action plans, including building and strengthening core competencies?
<--- Score

29. Are you measuring, monitoring and predicting Service Applications activities to optimize operations and profitability, and enhancing outcomes?
<--- Score

30. Is there a transfer of ownership and knowledge to process owner and process team tasked with the responsibilities.
<--- Score

31. You may have created your quality measures at a time when you lacked resources, technology wasn't up to the required standard, or low service levels were the industry norm. Have those circumstances changed?
<--- Score

32. Is there documentation that will support the successful operation of the improvement?
<--- Score

33. Who is going to spread your message?
<--- Score

34. Who sets the Service Applications standards?
<--- Score

35. How can you best use all of your knowledge repositories to enhance learning and sharing?
<--- Score

36. What do you stand for--and what are you against?
<--- Score

37. What is the standard for acceptable Service Applications performance?
<--- Score

38. Are the Service Applications standards challenging?
<--- Score

39. How do you select, collect, align, and integrate Service Applications data and information for tracking daily operations and overall organizational performance, including progress relative to strategic objectives and action plans?
<--- Score

40. Are controls in place and consistently applied?
<--- Score

41. What are the performance and scale of the Service Applications tools?
<--- Score

42. Will any special training be provided for results interpretation?
<--- Score

43. Does Service Applications appropriately measure and monitor risk?
<--- Score

44. What Service Applications standards are applicable?
<--- Score

45. Are there documented procedures?
<--- Score

46. How will the process owner and team be able to hold the gains?
<--- Score

47. How will the day-to-day responsibilities for monitoring and continual improvement be

transferred from the improvement team to the process owner?

<--- Score

48. What are the key elements of your Service Applications performance improvement system, including your evaluation, organizational learning, and innovation processes?

<--- Score

49. Who is the Service Applications process owner?

<--- Score

50. What should you measure to verify efficiency gains?

<--- Score

51. Does job training on the documented procedures need to be part of the process team's education and training?

<--- Score

52. What is the recommended frequency of auditing?

<--- Score

53. Is there an action plan in case of emergencies?

<--- Score

54. Has the improved process and its steps been standardized?

<--- Score

55. What is your plan to assess your security risks?

<--- Score

56. What are you attempting to measure/monitor?

<--- Score

57. What is the control/monitoring plan?
<--- Score

58. Has the Service Applications value of standards been quantified?
<--- Score

59. What adjustments to the strategies are needed?
<--- Score

60. Is new knowledge gained imbedded in the response plan?
<--- Score

61. How do you plan for the cost of succession?
<--- Score

62. Is knowledge gained on process shared and institutionalized?
<--- Score

63. How do you monitor usage and cost?
<--- Score

64. Can you adapt and adjust to changing Service Applications situations?
<--- Score

65. How do you plan on providing proper recognition and disclosure of supporting companies?
<--- Score

66. What are the critical parameters to watch?
<--- Score

67. Where do ideas that reach policy makers and planners as proposals for Service Applications strengthening and reform actually originate?
<--- Score

68. Who controls critical resources?
<--- Score

69. What do you measure to verify effectiveness gains?
<--- Score

70. How do you encourage people to take control and responsibility?
<--- Score

71. How do controls support value?
<--- Score

72. Is a response plan established and deployed?
<--- Score

73. What key inputs and outputs are being measured on an ongoing basis?
<--- Score

74. How is change control managed?
<--- Score

75. Is there a control plan in place for sustaining improvements (short and long-term)?
<--- Score

76. How will the process owner verify improvement in present and future sigma levels, process capabilities?

<--- Score

77. What do your reports reflect?
<--- Score

78. Do the Service Applications decisions you make today help people and the planet tomorrow?
<--- Score

79. Are documented procedures clear and easy to follow for the operators?
<--- Score

80. Implementation Planning: is a pilot needed to test the changes before a full roll out occurs?
<--- Score

81. What are the known security controls?
<--- Score

82. Is reporting being used or needed?
<--- Score

83. Do you monitor the effectiveness of your Service Applications activities?
<--- Score

84. Do the viable solutions scale to future needs?
<--- Score

85. Is there a documented and implemented monitoring plan?
<--- Score

86. Are pertinent alerts monitored, analyzed and distributed to appropriate personnel?

<--- Score

87. Will your goals reflect your program budget?
<--- Score

88. How will Service Applications decisions be made and monitored?
<--- Score

89. Who will be in control?
<--- Score

90. Against what alternative is success being measured?
<--- Score

91. Are new process steps, standards, and documentation ingrained into normal operations?
<--- Score

92. What quality tools were useful in the control phase?
<--- Score

93. Are the planned controls in place?
<--- Score

94. How do your controls stack up?
<--- Score

95. Have new or revised work instructions resulted?
<--- Score

96. How will new or emerging customer needs/ requirements be checked/communicated to orient the process toward meeting the new specifications

and continually reducing variation?
<--- Score

97. Is there a recommended audit plan for routine surveillance inspections of Service Applications's gains?
<--- Score

98. Are suggested corrective/restorative actions indicated on the response plan for known causes to problems that might surface?
<--- Score

Add up total points for this section:
_ _ _ _ _ = Total points for this section

Divided by: _ _ _ _ _ _ (number of statements answered) = _ _ _ _ _ _
Average score for this section

Transfer your score to the Service Applications Index at the beginning of the Self-Assessment.

CRITERION #7: SUSTAIN:

INTENT: Retain the benefits.

In my belief, the answer to this question is clearly defined:

5 Strongly Agree

4 Agree

3 Neutral

2 Disagree

1 Strongly Disagree

1. What is it like to work for you?
<--- Score

2. What new services of functionality will be implemented next with Service Applications ?
<--- Score

3. How is implementation research currently incorporated into each of your goals?
<--- Score

4. Is the Service Applications organization completing tasks effectively and efficiently?
<--- Score

5. Who are your customers?
<--- Score

6. How do you ensure that implementations of Service Applications products are done in a way that ensures safety?
<--- Score

7. What are you trying to prove to yourself, and how might it be hijacking your life and business success?
<--- Score

8. What happens at your organization when people fail?
<--- Score

9. What is your question? Why?
<--- Score

10. Do you think Service Applications accomplishes the goals you expect it to accomplish?
<--- Score

11. How do you cross-sell and up-sell your Service Applications success?
<--- Score

12. How do you foster the skills, knowledge, talents, attributes, and characteristics you want to have?
<--- Score

13. Do you see more potential in people than they do

in themselves?
<--- Score

14. What Service Applications skills are most important?
<--- Score

15. Political -is anyone trying to undermine this project?
<--- Score

16. When information truly is ubiquitous, when reach and connectivity are completely global, when computing resources are infinite, and when a whole new set of impossibilities are not only possible, but happening, what will that do to your business?
<--- Score

17. Who are the key stakeholders?
<--- Score

18. Do you say no to customers for no reason?
<--- Score

19. What are the potential basics of Service Applications fraud?
<--- Score

20. How are you engineering LaaS-service applications for this?
<--- Score

21. How can you incorporate support to ensure safe and effective use of Service Applications into the services that you provide?
<--- Score

22. How much does Service Applications help?
<--- Score

23. Why not do Service Applications?
<--- Score

24. What are the barriers to increased Service Applications production?
<--- Score

25. Are the criteria for selecting recommendations stated?
<--- Score

26. What would you recommend your friend do if he/she were facing this dilemma?
<--- Score

27. Do you have the right capabilities and capacities?
<--- Score

28. How likely is it that a customer would recommend your company to a friend or colleague?
<--- Score

29. Why do and why don't your customers like your organization?
<--- Score

30. Who do you think the world wants your organization to be?
<--- Score

31. Will there be any necessary staff changes (redundancies or new hires)?

<--- Score

32. How do you deal with Service Applications changes?
<--- Score

33. What is the funding source for this project?
<--- Score

34. What is the estimated value of the project?
<--- Score

35. How do you listen to customers to obtain actionable information?
<--- Score

36. Who is responsible for errors?
<--- Score

37. Who are four people whose careers you have enhanced?
<--- Score

38. If you had to leave your organization for a year and the only communication you could have with employees/colleagues was a single paragraph, what would you write?
<--- Score

39. Is there any reason to believe the opposite of my current belief?
<--- Score

40. Are you using a design thinking approach and integrating Innovation, Service Applications Experience, and Brand Value?

<--- Score

41. How do you proactively clarify deliverables and Service Applications quality expectations?
<--- Score

42. Are you changing as fast as the world around you?
<--- Score

43. Did your employees make progress today?
<--- Score

44. What is the recommended frequency of auditing?
<--- Score

45. Are you / should you be revolutionary or evolutionary?
<--- Score

46. Do you feel that more should be done in the Service Applications area?
<--- Score

47. Ask yourself: how would you do this work if you only had one staff member to do it?
<--- Score

48. What have you done to protect your business from competitive encroachment?
<--- Score

49. Who uses your product in ways you never expected?
<--- Score

50. Instead of going to current contacts for new ideas,

what if you reconnected with dormant contacts--
the people you used to know? If you were going
reactivate a dormant tie, who would it be?
<--- Score

51. Why should people listen to you?
<--- Score

52. What is the source of the strategies for Service
Applications strengthening and reform?
<--- Score

53. What are internal and external Service
Applications relations?
<--- Score

54. What is your formula for success in Service
Applications ?
<--- Score

55. What are the top 3 things at the forefront of your
Service Applications agendas for the next 3 years?
<--- Score

56. If you do not follow, then how to lead?
<--- Score

57. How important is Service Applications to the user
organizations mission?
<--- Score

58. What trophy do you want on your mantle?
<--- Score

59. Do you have an implicit bias for capital
investments over people investments?

<--- Score

60. What is the kind of project structure that would be appropriate for your Service Applications project, should it be formal and complex, or can it be less formal and relatively simple?
<--- Score

61. If you weren't already in this business, would you enter it today? And if not, what are you going to do about it?
<--- Score

62. How are you engineering Augmented Reality-service applications for this?
<--- Score

63. What you are going to do to affect the numbers?
<--- Score

64. Can you maintain your growth without detracting from the factors that have contributed to your success?
<--- Score

65. Can you do all this work?
<--- Score

66. What have been your experiences in defining long range Service Applications goals?
<--- Score

67. Is there any existing Service Applications governance structure?
<--- Score

68. In a project to restructure Service Applications outcomes, which stakeholders would you involve?
<--- Score

69. Who have you, as a company, historically been when you've been at your best?
<--- Score

70. What must you excel at?
<--- Score

71. What could happen if you do not do it?
<--- Score

72. Whom among your colleagues do you trust, and for what?
<--- Score

73. How do you keep the momentum going?
<--- Score

74. What trouble can you get into?
<--- Score

75. How can you become more high-tech but still be high touch?
<--- Score

76. In retrospect, of the projects that you pulled the plug on, what percent do you wish had been allowed to keep going, and what percent do you wish had ended earlier?
<--- Score

77. Operational - will it work?
<--- Score

78. How do you determine the key elements that affect Service Applications workforce satisfaction, how are these elements determined for different workforce groups and segments?
<--- Score

79. Do you think you know, or do you know you know ?
<--- Score

80. What Service Applications modifications can you make work for you?
<--- Score

81. How do you make it meaningful in connecting Service Applications with what users do day-to-day?
<--- Score

82. What stupid rule would you most like to kill?
<--- Score

83. How do you provide a safe environment -physically and emotionally?
<--- Score

84. What may be the consequences for the performance of an organization if all stakeholders are not consulted regarding Service Applications?
<--- Score

85. What is an unauthorized commitment?
<--- Score

86. Who will manage the integration of tools?
<--- Score

87. Are all key stakeholders present at all Structured Walkthroughs?
<--- Score

88. To whom do you add value?
<--- Score

89. Who will provide the final approval of Service Applications deliverables?
<--- Score

90. What is effective Service Applications?
<--- Score

91. How do you maintain Service Applications's Integrity?
<--- Score

92. Is a Service Applications team work effort in place?
<--- Score

93. What are the usability implications of Service Applications actions?
<--- Score

94. What is the overall talent health of your organization as a whole at senior levels, and for each organization reporting to a member of the Senior Leadership Team?
<--- Score

95. Which Service Applications goals are the most important?
<--- Score

96. Is Service Applications dependent on the successful delivery of a current project?
<--- Score

97. How do you track customer value, profitability or financial return, organizational success, and sustainability?
<--- Score

98. Who do we want your customers to become?
<--- Score

99. What role does communication play in the success or failure of a Service Applications project?
<--- Score

100. How do you know if you are successful?
<--- Score

101. Is Service Applications realistic, or are you setting yourself up for failure?
<--- Score

102. At what moment would you think; Will I get fired?
<--- Score

103. What management system can you use to leverage the Service Applications experience, ideas, and concerns of the people closest to the work to be done?
<--- Score

104. How do you create buy-in?
<--- Score

105. Whose voice (department, ethnic group, women,

older workers, etc) might you have missed hearing from in your company, and how might you amplify this voice to create positive momentum for your business?

<--- Score

106. How will you know that the Service Applications project has been successful?

<--- Score

107. If you got fired and a new hire took your place, what would she do different?

<--- Score

108. What are specific Service Applications rules to follow?

<--- Score

109. How can you become the company that would put you out of business?

<--- Score

110. Who else should you help?

<--- Score

111. What relationships among Service Applications trends do you perceive?

<--- Score

112. How do you transition from the baseline to the target?

<--- Score

113. What happens if you do not have enough funding?

<--- Score

114. How will you motivate the stakeholders with the least vested interest?

<--- Score

115. Are you satisfied with your current role? If not, what is missing from it?

<--- Score

116. If you were responsible for initiating and implementing major changes in your organization, what steps might you take to ensure acceptance of those changes?

<--- Score

117. What are the business goals Service Applications is aiming to achieve?

<--- Score

118. Who will be responsible for deciding whether Service Applications goes ahead or not after the initial investigations?

<--- Score

119. If you find that you havent accomplished one of the goals for one of the steps of the Service Applications strategy, what will you do to fix it?

<--- Score

120. What projects are going on in the organization today, and what resources are those projects using from the resource pools?

<--- Score

121. What are the gaps in your knowledge and experience?

<--- Score

122. How do you stay inspired?
<--- Score

123. Marketing budgets are tighter, consumers are more skeptical, and social media has changed forever the way we talk about Service Applications, how do you gain traction?
<--- Score

124. Has implementation been effective in reaching specified objectives so far?
<--- Score

125. Think of your Service Applications project, what are the main functions?
<--- Score

126. What goals did you miss?
<--- Score

127. What potential megatrends could make your business model obsolete?
<--- Score

128. What are strategies for increasing support and reducing opposition?
<--- Score

129. What are the short and long-term Service Applications goals?
<--- Score

130. Do you have enough freaky customers in your portfolio pushing you to the limit day in and day out?

<--- Score

131. If you had to rebuild your organization without any traditional competitive advantages (i.e., no killer technology, promising research, innovative product/ service delivery model, etcetera), how would your people have to approach their work and collaborate together in order to create the necessary conditions for success?
<--- Score

132. If your company went out of business tomorrow, would anyone who doesn't get a paycheck here care?
<--- Score

133. Do Service Applications rules make a reasonable demand on a users capabilities?
<--- Score

134. Are you maintaining a past–present–future perspective throughout the Service Applications discussion?
<--- Score

135. Which functions and people interact with the supplier and or customer?
<--- Score

136. Is your strategy driving your strategy? Or is the way in which you allocate resources driving your strategy?
<--- Score

137. Who do you want your customers to become?
<--- Score

138. Is your basic point _____ or _____?
<--- Score

139. What are the key enablers to make this Service Applications move?
<--- Score

140. If your customer were your grandmother, would you tell her to buy what you're selling?
<--- Score

141. Is there a work around that you can use?
<--- Score

142. Are the assumptions believable and achievable?
<--- Score

143. What one word do you want to own in the minds of your customers, employees, and partners?
<--- Score

144. Who is on the team?
<--- Score

145. What is your competitive advantage?
<--- Score

146. What is the overall business strategy?
<--- Score

147. What is your Service Applications strategy?
<--- Score

148. How do you foster innovation?
<--- Score

149. What are the success criteria that will indicate that Service Applications objectives have been met and the benefits delivered?
<--- Score

150. Are assumptions made in Service Applications stated explicitly?
<--- Score

151. Why will customers want to buy your organizations products/services?
<--- Score

152. What information is critical to your organization that your executives are ignoring?
<--- Score

153. Is maximizing Service Applications protection the same as minimizing Service Applications loss?
<--- Score

154. How do you go about securing Service Applications?
<--- Score

155. Who, on the executive team or the board, has spoken to a customer recently?
<--- Score

156. What did you miss in the interview for the worst hire you ever made?
<--- Score

157. How do you engage the workforce, in addition to satisfying them?
<--- Score

158. Will it be accepted by users?
<--- Score

159. How do you assess the Service Applications pitfalls that are inherent in implementing it?
<--- Score

160. How do you accomplish your long range Service Applications goals?
<--- Score

161. How will you ensure you get what you expected?
<--- Score

162. How can you negotiate Service Applications successfully with a stubborn boss, an irate client, or a deceitful coworker?
<--- Score

163. How will you insure seamless interoperability of Service Applications moving forward?
<--- Score

164. If there were zero limitations, what would you do differently?
<--- Score

165. How are you doing compared to your industry?
<--- Score

166. How do customers see your organization?
<--- Score

167. Why is Service Applications important for you now?

<--- Score

168. Which models, tools and techniques are necessary?
<--- Score

169. How do you keep records, of what?
<--- Score

170. In the past year, what have you done (or could you have done) to increase the accurate perception of your company/brand as ethical and honest?
<--- Score

171. What are the challenges?
<--- Score

172. What is a feasible sequencing of reform initiatives over time?
<--- Score

173. How do you govern and fulfill your societal responsibilities?
<--- Score

174. Who is responsible for Service Applications?
<--- Score

175. What was the last experiment you ran?
<--- Score

176. Where can you break convention?
<--- Score

177. What business benefits will Service Applications goals deliver if achieved?

<--- Score

178. What are you challenging?
<--- Score

179. Are you making progress, and are you making progress as Service Applications leaders?
<--- Score

180. What is the purpose of Service Applications in relation to the mission?
<--- Score

181. Do you have the right people on the bus?
<--- Score

182. Is it economical; do you have the time and money?
<--- Score

183. How do you lead with Service Applications in mind?
<--- Score

184. How much contingency will be available in the budget?
<--- Score

185. Would you rather sell to knowledgeable and informed customers or to uninformed customers?
<--- Score

186. What does your signature ensure?
<--- Score

187. Who will determine interim and final deadlines?

<--- Score

188. What is the craziest thing you can do?
<--- Score

189. What should you stop doing?
<--- Score

190. What are the long-term Service Applications goals?
<--- Score

191. Are you relevant? Will you be relevant five years from now? Ten?
<--- Score

192. What are your most important goals for the strategic Service Applications objectives?
<--- Score

193. How long will it take to change?
<--- Score

194. What are the rules and assumptions your industry operates under? What if the opposite were true?
<--- Score

195. What threat is Service Applications addressing?
<--- Score

196. What is something you believe that nearly no one agrees with you on?
<--- Score

197. What unique value proposition (UVP) do you offer?

<--- Score

198. What are the essentials of internal Service
Applications management?
<--- Score

199. What counts that you are not counting?
<--- Score

Add up total points for this section:
_____ = Total points for this section

Divided by: _____ (number of
statements answered) = _____
Average score for this section

Transfer your score to the Service
Applications Index at the beginning of
the Self-Assessment.

Service Applications and Managing Projects, Criteria for Project Managers:

1.0 Initiating Process Group: Service Applications

1. How will it affect me?

2. When must it be done?

3. How can you make your needs known?

4. What were things that you did well, and could improve, and how?

5. When will the Service Applications project be done?

6. What are the tools and techniques to be used in each phase?

7. Where must it be done?

8. How will you know you did it?

9. What is the NEXT thing to do?

10. Were decisions made in a timely manner?

11. What are the required resources?

12. What will be the pressing issues of tomorrow?

13. At which cmmi level are software processes documented, standardized, and integrated into a standard to-be practiced process for your organization?

14. What are the constraints?

15. First of all, should any action be taken?

16. Were resources available as planned?

17. What were things that you did very well and want to do the same again on the next Service Applications project?

18. How well defined and documented were the Service Applications project management processes you chose to use?

19. What must be done?

20. What communication items need improvement?

1.1 Project Charter: Service Applications

21. What are the assumptions?

22. Does the Service Applications project need to consider any special capacity or capability issues?

23. Why do you need to manage scope?

24. Customer benefits: what customer requirements does this Service Applications project address?

25. Major high-level milestone targets: what events measure progress?

26. When is a charter needed?

27. When do you use a Service Applications project Charter?

28. Who manages integration?

29. What is the purpose of the Service Applications project?

30. Review the general mission What system will be affected by the improvement efforts?

31. Run it as as a startup?

32. Why Outsource?

33. What are you striving to accomplish (measurable goal(s))?

34. Why executive support?

35. What ideas do you have for initial tests of change (PDSA cycles)?

36. Service Applications project objective statement: what must the Service Applications project do?

37. Name and describe the elements that deal with providing the detail?

38. What are the assigned resources?

39. Environmental stewardship and sustainability considerations: what is the process that will be used to ensure compliance with the environmental stewardship policy?

40. Who is the sponsor?

1.2 Stakeholder Register: Service Applications

41. How big is the gap?

42. What is the power of the stakeholder?

43. Who wants to talk about Security?

44. How should employers make voices heard?

45. Who are the stakeholders?

46. How much influence do they have on the Service Applications project?

47. Is your organization ready for change?

48. What are the major Service Applications project milestones requiring communications or providing communications opportunities?

49. Who is managing stakeholder engagement?

50. What & Why?

51. What opportunities exist to provide communications?

52. How will reports be created?

1.3 Stakeholder Analysis Matrix: Service Applications

53. Volumes, production, economies?

54. Contributions to policy and practice?

55. Legislative effects?

56. Timescales, deadlines and pressures?

57. What do you need to appraise?

58. Guiding question: who shall you involve in the making of the stakeholder map?

59. Why involve the stakeholder?

60. Where are mitigation costs factored in?

61. How can you fill the need to show progress?

62. Inoculations or payment to receive them?

63. Identify the stakeholders levels most frequently used –or at least sought– in your Service Applications projects and for which purpose?

64. Are there two or three that rise to the top, and a couple that are sliding to the bottom?

65. Political effects?

66. How to measure the achievement of the Immediate Objective?

67. Seasonality, weather effects?

68. Opponents; who are the opponents?

69. Economy - home, abroad?

70. Cashflow, start-up cash-drain?

71. Do the stakeholders goals and expectations support or conflict with the Service Applications project goals?

72. What is your Risk Management?

2.0 Planning Process Group: Service Applications

73. Are the follow-up indicators relevant and do they meet the quality needed to measure the outputs and outcomes of the Service Applications project?

74. How will it affect you?

75. Are you just doing busywork to pass the time?

76. How well defined and documented are the Service Applications project management processes you chose to use?

77. If a risk event occurs, what will you do?

78. To what extent are the visions and actions of the partners consistent or divergent with regard to the program?

79. What input will you be required to provide the Service Applications project team?

80. To what extent are the participating departments coordinating with each other?

81. How should needs be met?

82. To what extent have the target population and participants made the activities own, taking an active role in it?

83. You did your readings, yes?

84. Have more efficient (sensitive) and appropriate measures been adopted to respond to the political and socio-cultural problems identified?

85. Professionals want to know what is expected from them; what are the deliverables?

86. Have operating capacities been created and/or reinforced in partners?

87. Just how important is your work to the overall success of the Service Applications project?

88. If you are late, will anybody notice?

89. Are work methodologies, financial instruments, etc. shared among departments, organizations and Service Applications projects?

90. Will you be replaced?

91. How does activity resource estimation affect activity duration estimation?

2.1 Project Management Plan: Service Applications

92. When is a Service Applications project management plan created?

93. What data/reports/tools/etc. do your PMs need?

94. Are comparable cost estimates used for comparing, screening and selecting alternative plans, and has a reasonable cost estimate been developed for the recommended plan?

95. What would you do differently?

96. What are the training needs?

97. What is risk management?

98. Who is the Service Applications project Manager?

99. What are the known stakeholder requirements?

100. Is the appropriate plan selected based on your organizations objectives and evaluation criteria expressed in Principles and Guidelines policies?

101. Why do you manage integration?

102. How do you organize the costs in the Service Applications project management plan?

103. Is mitigation authorized or recommended?

104. What is the justification?

105. How well are you able to manage your risk?

106. Has the selected plan been formulated using cost effectiveness and incremental analysis techniques?

107. What would you do differently what did not work?

108. What did not work so well?

109. Do there need to be organizational changes?

110. What should you drop in order to add something new?

2.2 Scope Management Plan: Service Applications

111. Is there a scope management plan that includes how Service Applications project scope will be defined, developed, monitored, validated and controlled?

112. Is the assigned Service Applications project manager a PMP (Certified Service Applications project manager) and experienced?

113. What strengths do you have?

114. Has the Service Applications project manager been identified?

115. Is current scope of the Service Applications project substantially different than that originally defined?

116. Are Service Applications project leaders committed to this Service Applications project full time?

117. Are changes in scope (deliverable commitments) agreed to by all affected groups & individuals?

118. Describe how the deliverables will be verified against the Service Applications project scope. To whom will the deliverables be first presented for inspection and verification?

119. Have reserves been created to address risks?

120. Assess the expected stability of the scope of this Service Applications project how likely is it to change, how frequently, and by how much?

121. To whom will the deliverables be first presented for inspection and verification?

122. Do you have funding for Service Applications project and product development, implementation and on-going support?

123. Have the procedures for identifying budget variances been followed?

124. What is the estimated cost of creating and implementing?

125. Are updated Service Applications project time & resource estimates reasonable based on the current Service Applications project stage?

126. Is there an approved case?

127. Have Service Applications project success criteria been defined?

128. Are the quality tools and methods identified in the Quality Plan appropriate to the Service Applications project?

2.3 Requirements Management Plan: Service Applications

129. How knowledgeable is the primary Stakeholder(s) in the proposed application area?

130. Who will finally present the work or product(s) for acceptance?

131. Will you have access to stakeholders when you need them?

132. Is the system software (non-operating system) new to the IT Service Applications project team?

133. What cost metrics will be used?

134. Has the requirements team been instructed in the Change Control process?

135. Is the system software (non-operating system) new to the IT Service Applications project team?

136. How will bidders price evaluations be done, by deliverables, phases, or in a big bang?

137. What is a problem?

138. How knowledgeable is the team in the proposed application area?

139. To see if a requirement statement is sufficiently well-defined, read it from the developers perspective.

Mentally add the phrase, call me when youre done to the end of the requirement and see if that makes you nervous. In other words, would you need additional clarification from the author to understand the requirement well enough to design and implement it?

140. Will you document changes to requirements?

141. How will requirements be managed?

142. Who has the authority to reject Service Applications project requirements?

143. How will you communicate scheduled tasks to other team members?

144. Who will initially review the Service Applications project work or products to ensure it meets the applicable acceptance criteria?

145. Did you provide clear and concise specifications?

146. Describe the process for rejecting the Service Applications project requirements. Who has the authority to reject Service Applications project requirements?

147. Is requirements work dependent on any other specific Service Applications project or non-Service Applications project activities (e.g. funding, approvals, procurement)?

148. Did you get proper approvals?

2.4 Requirements Documentation: Service Applications

149. Where do you define what is a customer, what are the attributes of customer?

150. What can tools do for us?

151. How much does requirements engineering cost?

152. What will be the integration problems?

153. Do your constraints stand?

154. What if the system wasn t implemented?

155. Basic work/business process; high-level, what is being touched?

156. Where do system and software requirements come from, what are sources?

157. Is new technology needed?

158. What are the attributes of a customer?

159. What images does it conjure?

160. Validity. does the system provide the functions which best support the customers needs?

161. How to document system requirements?

162. What is the risk associated with the technology?

163. Who is interacting with the system?

164. Are all functions required by the customer included?

165. Can the requirement be changed without a large impact on other requirements?

166. What variations exist for a process?

167. Has requirements gathering uncovered information that would necessitate changes?

168. What kind of entity is a problem ?

2.5 Requirements Traceability Matrix: Service Applications

169. How small is small enough?

170. What is the WBS?

171. What are the chronologies, contingencies, consequences, criteria?

172. How do you manage scope?

173. Why use a WBS?

174. Will you use a Requirements Traceability Matrix?

175. Describe the process for approving requirements so they can be added to the traceability matrix and Service Applications project work can be performed. Will the Service Applications project requirements become approved in writing?

176. What percentage of Service Applications projects are producing traceability matrices between requirements and other work products?

177. Why do you manage scope?

178. Is there a requirements traceability process in place?

179. How will it affect the stakeholders personally in career?

180. Do you have a clear understanding of all subcontracts in place?

2.6 Project Scope Statement: Service Applications

181. Risks?

182. Is the Service Applications project organization documented and on file?

183. What is the most common tool for helping define the detail?

184. Will you need a statement of work?

185. Have the reports to be produced, distributed, and filed been defined?

186. Elements of scope management that deal with concept development ?

187. Is the Service Applications project manager qualified and experienced in Service Applications project management?

188. What process would you recommend for creating the Service Applications project scope statement?

189. Is there an information system for the Service Applications project?

190. Service Applications project lead, team lead, solution architect?

191. What are the possible consequences should a risk

come to occur?

192. Were potential customers involved early in the planning process?

193. Is the scope of your Service Applications project well defined?

194. Will tasks be marked complete only after QA has been successfully completed?

195. Who will you recommend approve the change, and when do you recommend the change reviews occur?

196. Was planning completed before the Service Applications project was initiated?

197. Will the risk plan be updated on a regular and frequent basis?

198. Is this process communicated to the customer and team members?

199. Are there specific processes you will use to evaluate and approve/reject changes?

2.7 Assumption and Constraint Log: Service Applications

200. Contradictory information between different documents?

201. Does the traceability documentation describe the tool and/or mechanism to be used to capture traceability throughout the life cycle?

202. Are there nonconformance issues?

203. Should factors be unpredictable over time?

204. What do you audit?

205. Does the document/deliverable meet general requirements (for example, statement of work) for all deliverables?

206. Do you know what your customers expectations are regarding this process?

207. Is the steering committee active in Service Applications project oversight?

208. Does the Service Applications project have a formal Service Applications project Plan?

209. What if failure during recovery?

210. Do the requirements meet the standards of correctness, completeness, consistency, accuracy, and

readability?

211. What other teams / processes would be impacted by changes to the current process, and how?

212. Are there processes defining how software will be developed including development methods, overall timeline for development, software product standards, and traceability?

213. What do you log?

214. What weaknesses do you have?

215. How relevant is this attribute to this Service Applications project or audit?

216. Does the document/deliverable meet all requirements (for example, statement of work) specific to this deliverable?

217. How many Service Applications project staff does this specific process affect?

218. Violation trace: why ?

2.8 Work Breakdown Structure: Service Applications

219. How much detail?

220. When do you stop?

221. Is it still viable?

222. What is the probability of completing the Service Applications project in less that xx days?

223. Why would you develop a Work Breakdown Structure?

224. Who has to do it?

225. How many levels?

226. When does it have to be done?

227. How big is a work-package?

228. How far down?

229. Where does it take place?

230. When would you develop a Work Breakdown Structure?

231. Can you make it?

232. Why is it useful?

233. What is the probability that the Service Applications project duration will exceed xx weeks?

234. Is the work breakdown structure (wbs) defined and is the scope of the Service Applications project clear with assigned deliverable owners?

235. Do you need another level?

236. Is it a change in scope?

2.9 WBS Dictionary: Service Applications

237. Where engineering standards or other internal work measurement systems are used, is there a formal relationship between corresponding values and work package budgets?

238. Evaluate the performance of operating organizations?

239. What went wrong?

240. Are the wbs and organizational levels for application of the Service Applications projected overhead costs identified?

241. Do work packages reflect the actual way in which the work will be done and are they meaningful products or management-oriented subdivisions of a higher level element of work?

242. Are the requirements for all items of overhead established by rational, traceable processes?

243. Where learning is used in developing underlying budgets is there a direct relationship between anticipated learning and time phased budgets?

244. Are the latest revised estimates of costs at completion compared with the established budgets at appropriate levels and causes of variances identified?

245. Are the contractors estimates of costs at completion reconcilable with cost data reported to us?

246. Does the contractors system provide unit costs, equivalent unit or lot costs in terms of labor, material, other direct, and indirect costs?

247. Is all budget available as management reserve identified and excluded from the performance measurement baseline?

248. Are current work performance indicators and goals relatable to original goals as modified by contractual changes, replanning, and reprogramming actions?

249. Are the overhead pools formally and adequately identified?

250. Are indirect costs charged to the appropriate indirect pools and incurring organization?

251. Are the variances between budgeted and actual indirect costs identified and analyzed at the level of assigned responsibility for control (indirect pool, department, etc.)?

252. Are retroactive changes to budgets for completed work specifically prohibited in an established procedure, and is this procedure adhered to?

253. Changes in the overhead pool and/or organization structures?

254. Changes in the direct base to which overhead costs are allocated?

2.10 Schedule Management Plan: Service Applications

255. Were stakeholders aware and supportive of the principles and practices of modern software estimation?

256. Does the business case include how the Service Applications project aligns with your organizations strategic goals & objectives?

257. Are risk triggers captured?

258. Was your organizations estimating methodology being used and followed?

259. Has the ims been resource-loaded and are assigned resources reasonable and available?

260. Are meeting minutes captured and sent out after the meeting?

261. Are adequate resources provided for the quality assurance function?

262. Do all stakeholders know how to access this repository and where to find the Service Applications project documentation?

263. Have key stakeholders been identified?

264. Has process improvement efforts been completed before requirements efforts begin?

265. Are Service Applications project contact logs kept up to date?

266. Are procurement deliverables arriving on time and to specification?

267. Is documentation created for communication with the suppliers and Vendors?

268. Time for overtime?

269. Is Service Applications project status reviewed with the steering and executive teams at appropriate intervals?

270. Does the detailed work plan match the complexity of tasks with the capabilities of personnel?

271. What will be the final cost of the Service Applications project if status quo is maintained?

272. Has the Service Applications project scope been baselined?

273. Are software metrics formally captured, analyzed and used as a basis for other Service Applications project estimates?

274. Is there a set of procedures defining the scope, procedures, and deliverables defining quality control?

2.11 Activity List: Service Applications

275. What will be performed?

276. How will it be performed?

277. What is the LF and LS for each activity?

278. Are the required resources available or need to be acquired?

279. What did not go as well?

280. Can you determine the activity that must finish, before this activity can start?

281. How much slack is available in the Service Applications project?

282. What are you counting on?

283. The wbs is developed as part of a joint planning session. and how do you know that youhave done this right?

284. How can the Service Applications project be displayed graphically to better visualize the activities?

285. What is the total time required to complete the Service Applications project if no delays occur?

286. How detailed should a Service Applications project get?

287. How difficult will it be to do specific activities on this Service Applications project?

288. Where will it be performed?

289. How do you determine the late start (LS) for each activity?

290. What went right?

291. What are the critical bottleneck activities?

292. What went well?

293. Should you include sub-activities?

2.12 Activity Attributes: Service Applications

294. Does your organization of the data change its meaning?

295. Why?

296. What is the general pattern here?

297. Has management defined a definite timeframe for the turnaround or Service Applications project window?

298. How difficult will it be to complete specific activities on this Service Applications project?

299. Activity: what is Missing?

300. Were there other ways you could have organized the data to achieve similar results?

301. What is your organizations history in doing similar activities?

302. Where else does it apply?

303. Do you feel very comfortable with your prediction?

304. How else could the items be grouped?

305. How many resources do you need to complete

the work scope within a limit of X number of days?

306. How many days do you need to complete the work scope with a limit of X number of resources?

307. Activity: fair or not fair?

308. Have constraints been applied to the start and finish milestones for the phases?

309. Can more resources be added?

310. What is missing?

311. Activity: what is In the Bag?

312. Resources to accomplish the work?

313. Resource is assigned to?

2.13 Milestone List: Service Applications

314. Level of the Innovation?

315. Describe the concept of the technology, product or service that will be or has been developed. How will it be used?

316. How soon can the activity start?

317. What date will the task finish?

318. How late can each activity be finished and started?

319. Sustainable financial backing?

320. Sustaining internal capabilities?

321. Can you derive how soon can the whole Service Applications project finish?

322. Effects on core activities, distraction?

323. What specific improvements did you make to the Service Applications project proposal since the previous time?

324. What has been done so far?

325. Continuity, supply chain robustness?

326. How difficult will it be to do specific activities on this Service Applications project?

327. Information and research?

328. Gaps in capabilities?

329. Insurmountable weaknesses?

330. Milestone pages should display the UserID of the person who added the milestone. Does a report or query exist that provides this audit information?

2.14 Network Diagram: Service Applications

331. What is the probability of completing the Service Applications project in less that xx days?

332. What activity must be completed immediately before this activity can start?

333. Are you on time?

334. What activities must occur simultaneously with this activity?

335. Planning: who, how long, what to do?

336. If the Service Applications project network diagram cannot change and you have extra personnel resources, what is the BEST thing to do?

337. What controls the start and finish of a job?

338. Review the logical flow of the network diagram. Take a look at which activities you have first and then sequence the activities. Do they make sense?

339. What job or jobs precede it?

340. Where do you schedule uncertainty time?

341. What are the Major Administrative Issues?

342. Are the gantt chart and/or network diagram

updated periodically and used to assess the overall Service Applications project timetable?

343. What to do and When?

344. Where do schedules come from?

345. What are the tools?

346. What is the lowest cost to complete this Service Applications project in xx weeks?

347. Which type of network diagram allows you to depict four types of dependencies?

348. What job or jobs could run concurrently?

349. Exercise: what is the probability that the Service Applications project duration will exceed xx weeks?

2.15 Activity Resource Requirements: Service Applications

350. How do you handle petty cash?

351. Do you use tools like decomposition and rolling-wave planning to produce the activity list and other outputs?

352. Organizational Applicability?

353. Are there unresolved issues that need to be addressed?

354. Other support in specific areas?

355. Why do you do that?

356. What are constraints that you might find during the Human Resource Planning process?

357. Anything else?

358. How do you manage time?

359. When does monitoring begin?

360. How many signatures do you require on a check and does this match what is in your policy and procedures?

361. What is the Work Plan Standard?

362. Is there anything planned that does not need to be here?

363. Which logical relationship does the PDM use most often?

2.16 Resource Breakdown Structure: Service Applications

364. Goals for the Service Applications project. What is each stakeholders desired outcome for the Service Applications project?

365. When do they need the information?

366. Who delivers the information?

367. Are the required resources available?

368. What can you do to improve productivity?

369. Why do you do it?

370. Who needs what information?

371. Which resource planning tool provides information on resource responsibility and accountability?

372. What is the difference between % Complete and % work?

373. What defines a successful Service Applications project?

374. Any changes from stakeholders?

375. What is the primary purpose of the human resource plan?

376. What are the requirements for resource data?

377. Why is this important?

378. Which resources should be in the resource pool?

379. Changes based on input from stakeholders?

380. How difficult will it be to do specific activities on this Service Applications project?

2.17 Activity Duration Estimates: Service Applications

381. Does a process exist for approving or rejecting changes?

382. Are team building activities completed to improve team performance?

383. What are the ways to create and distribute Service Applications project performance information?

384. What is the duration of the critical path for this Service Applications project?

385. What is the career outlook for Service Applications project managers in information technology?

386. Which skills do you think are most important for an information technology Service Applications project manager?

387. Which tips for taking the PMP exam do you think would be most helpful for you?

388. What is the critical path for this Service Applications project and how long is it?

389. Do they make sense?

390. Research recruiting and retention strategies at

three different companies. What distinguishes one organization from another in this area?

391. Are procedures defined by which the Service Applications project scope may be changed?

392. What do corresponding sources say about Service Applications project management?

393. Have most organizations benefited from outsourcing?

394. Is risk identification completed regularly throughout the Service Applications project?

395. What are some general rules of thumb for deciding if cost variance, schedule variance, cost performance index, and schedule performance index numbers are good or bad?

396. Why do you think schedule issues often cause the most conflicts on Service Applications projects?

397. Which best describes how this affects the Service Applications project?

398. Will it help in finding or retaining employees?

399. What is involved in the solicitation process?

2.18 Duration Estimating Worksheet: Service Applications

400. What is cost and Service Applications project cost management?

401. Is this operation cost effective?

402. Why estimate costs?

403. Can the Service Applications project be constructed as planned?

404. How can the Service Applications project be displayed graphically to better visualize the activities?

405. Define the work as completely as possible. What work will be included in the Service Applications project?

406. Will the Service Applications project collaborate with the local community and leverage resources?

407. Does the Service Applications project provide innovative ways for stakeholders to overcome obstacles or deliver better outcomes?

408. Why estimate time and cost?

409. What info is needed?

410. Is the Service Applications project responsive to community need?

411. What work will be included in the Service Applications project?

412. Science = process: remember the scientific method?

413. What questions do you have?

414. Value pocket identification & quantification what are value pockets?

415. When does your organization expect to be able to complete it?

416. Do any colleagues have experience with your organization and/or RFPs?

417. What is your role?

2.19 Project Schedule: Service Applications

418. How do you know that youhave done this right?

419. How do you manage Service Applications project Risk?

420. What is Service Applications project management?

421. How detailed should a Service Applications project get?

422. If there are any qualifying green components to this Service Applications project, what portion of the total Service Applications project cost is green?

423. Eliminate unnecessary activities. Are there activities that came from a template or previous Service Applications project that are not applicable on this phase of this Service Applications project?

424. Are activities connected because logic dictates the order in which others occur?

425. Is the structure for tracking the Service Applications project schedule well defined and assigned to a specific individual?

426. Are procedures defined by which the Service Applications project schedule may be changed?

427. Did the Service Applications project come in under budget?

428. Why is this particularly bad?

429. What documents, if any, will the subcontractor provide (eg Service Applications project schedule, quality plan etc)?

430. Did the Service Applications project come in on schedule?

431. Is Service Applications project work proceeding in accordance with the original Service Applications project schedule?

432. Master Service Applications project schedule?

433. How can you minimize or control changes to Service Applications project schedules?

434. How can you fix it?

2.20 Cost Management Plan: Service Applications

435. Are the key elements of a Service Applications project Charter present?

436. Are metrics used to evaluate and manage Vendors?

437. Have activity relationships and interdependencies within tasks been adequately identified?

438. Is the assigned Service Applications project manager a PMP (Certified Service Applications project manager) and experienced?

439. Are internal Service Applications project status meetings held at reasonable intervals?

440. What are the nine areas of expertise?

441. Was the scope definition used in task sequencing?

442. Has a sponsor been identified?

443. Is there an onboarding process in place?

444. Is your organization certified as a supplier, wholesaler and/or regular dealer?

445. For cost control purposes?

446. Eac -estimate at completion, what is the total job expected to cost?

447. Scope of work – What is the scope of work for each of the planned contracts?

448. Why do you manage cost?

449. How relevant is this attribute to this Service Applications project or audit?

450. What is an Acceptance Management Process?

2.21 Activity Cost Estimates: Service Applications

451. How do you change activities?

452. What is the activity recast of the budget?

453. Did the consultant work with local staff to develop local capacity?

454. Performance bond should always provide what part of the contract value?

455. Padding is bad and contingencies are good. what is the difference?

456. If you are asked to lower your estimate because the price is too high, what are your options?

457. How do you fund change orders?

458. What is included in indirect cost being allocated?

459. Did the Service Applications project team have the right skills?

460. Were the tasks or work products prepared by the consultant useful?

461. Does the estimator estimate by task or by person?

462. What is the activity inventory?

463. What is procurement?

464. What is the estimators estimating history?

465. How do you treat administrative costs in the activity inventory?

466. What areas were overlooked on this Service Applications project?

467. Measurable - are the targets measurable?

468. Can you delete activities or make them inactive?

2.22 Cost Estimating Worksheet: Service Applications

469. Identify the timeframe necessary to monitor progress and collect data to determine how the selected measure has changed?

470. What additional Service Applications project(s) could be initiated as a result of this Service Applications project?

471. Is it feasible to establish a control group arrangement?

472. Can a trend be established from historical performance data on the selected measure and are the criteria for using trend analysis or forecasting methods met?

473. What happens to any remaining funds not used?

474. What will others want?

475. What can be included?

476. How will the results be shared and to whom?

477. Is the Service Applications project responsive to community need?

478. Who is best positioned to know and assist in identifying corresponding factors?

479. Does the Service Applications project provide innovative ways for stakeholders to overcome obstacles or deliver better outcomes?

480. Ask: are others positioned to know, are others credible, and will others cooperate?

481. What costs are to be estimated?

482. Will the Service Applications project collaborate with the local community and leverage resources?

483. What is the purpose of estimating?

484. What is the estimated labor cost today based upon this information?

2.23 Cost Baseline: Service Applications

485. Is request in line with priorities?

486. Does it impact schedule, cost, quality?

487. When should cost estimates be developed?

488. Review your risk triggers -have your risks changed?

489. Will the Service Applications project fail if the change request is not executed?

490. What is the reality?

491. How do you manage cost?

492. Is there anything unique in this Service Applications projects scope statement that will affect resources?

493. Does the suggested change request seem to represent a necessary enhancement to the product?

494. Has training and knowledge transfer of the operations organization been completed?

495. What is the consequence?

496. What is it ?

497. What is cost and Service Applications project cost management?

498. What is the most important thing to do next to make your Service Applications project successful?

499. Has the documentation relating to operation and maintenance of the product(s) or service(s) been delivered to, and accepted by, operations management?

500. Have all approved changes to the schedule baseline been identified and impact on the Service Applications project documented?

501. What deliverables come first?

2.24 Quality Management Plan: Service Applications

502. How will you know that a change is actually an improvement?

503. How do you prioritize?

504. How is staff trained on the recording of field notes?

505. What are you trying to accomplish?

506. How are your organizations compensation and recognition approaches and the performance management system used to reinforce high performance?

507. Who do you send data to?

508. What is quality planning ?

509. What is the Quality Management Plan?

510. Meet how often?

511. Are there procedures in place to effectively manage interdependencies with other Service Applications projects / systems?

512. Do the data quality objectives communicate the intended program need?

513. Who gets results of work?

514. Diagrams and tables to account for complex concepts and increase overall readability?

515. How does your organization recruit, hire, and retain new employees?

516. Is the process working, and people are not executing in compliance of the process?

517. Are there unnecessary steps that are creating bottlenecks and/or causing people to wait?

518. Is a component/condition present?

519. Are there processes in place to ensure internal consistency between the source code components?

520. What else should you do now?

2.25 Quality Metrics: Service Applications

521. Is there a set of procedures to capture, analyze and act on quality metrics?

522. Is quality culture a competitive advantage?

523. When will the Final Guidance will be issued?

524. Are documents on hand to provide explanations of privacy and confidentiality?

525. What level of statistical confidence do you use?

526. Were quality attributes reported?

527. How do you know if everyone is trying to improve the right things?

528. What approved evidence based screening tools can be used?

529. Has trace of defects been initiated?

530. How can the effectiveness of each of the activities be measured?

531. Can you correlate your quality metrics to profitability?

532. Is a risk containment plan in place?

533. What if the biggest risk to your business were the already stated people who do not complain?

534. How is it being measured?

535. How are requirements conflicts resolved?

536. Is material complete (and does it meet the standards)?

537. How does one achieve stability?

538. Should a modifier be included?

539. What forces exist that would cause them to change?

540. What can manufacturing professionals do to ensure quality is seen as an integral part of the entire product lifecycle?

2.26 Process Improvement Plan: Service Applications

541. Management commitment at all levels?

542. Has a process guide to collect the data been developed?

543. Are you making progress on the improvement framework?

544. Why quality management?

545. Does your process ensure quality?

546. What personnel are the sponsors for that initiative?

547. Everyone agrees on what process improvement is, right?

548. What is the test-cycle concept?

549. What makes people good SPI coaches?

550. How do you manage quality?

551. Where do you focus?

552. Have the frequency of collection and the points in the process where measurements will be made been determined?

553. What personnel are the champions for the initiative?

554. What is the return on investment?

555. Are you following the quality standards?

556. Where do you want to be?

557. Modeling current processes is great, and will you ever see a return on that investment?

558. Have storage and access mechanisms and procedures been determined?

2.27 Responsibility Assignment Matrix: Service Applications

559. Will too many Signing-off responsibilities delay the completion of the activity/deliverable?

560. Competencies and craftsmanship – what competencies are necessary and what level?

561. Are work packages assigned to performing organizations?

562. No rs: if a task has no one listed as responsible, who is getting the job done?

563. Do work packages consist of discrete tasks which are adequately described?

564. Who is the Service Applications project Manager?

565. Will too many Communicating responsibilities tangle the Service Applications project in unnecessary communications?

566. Time-phased control account budgets?

567. What simple tool can you use to help identify and prioritize Service Applications project risks that is very low tech and high touch?

568. Does the accounting system provide a basis for auditing records of direct costs chargeable to the contract?

569. How many hours by each staff member/rate?

570. Are material costs reported within the same period as that in which BCWP is earned for that material?

571. Evaluate the impact of schedule changes, work around, etc?

572. Contract line items and end items?

573. Wbs elements contractually specified for reporting of status (lowest level only)?

574. How many people do you need?

575. Actual cost of work performed?

576. Past experience – the person or the group worked at something similar in the past?

577. Is work progressively subdivided into detailed work packages as requirements are defined?

2.28 Roles and Responsibilities: Service Applications

578. Are Service Applications project team roles and responsibilities identified and documented?

579. Is there a training program in place for stakeholders covering expectations, roles and responsibilities and any addition knowledge others need to be good stakeholders?

580. Once the responsibilities are defined for the Service Applications project, have the deliverables, roles and responsibilities been clearly communicated to every participant?

581. Concern: where are you limited or have no authority, where you can not influence?

582. What expectations were met?

583. Are your budgets supportive of a culture of quality data?

584. What should you do now to ensure that you are meeting all expectations of your current position?

585. What should you do now to prepare yourself for a promotion, increased responsibilities or a different job?

586. How well did the Service Applications project Team understand the expectations of specific roles

and responsibilities?

587. Is the data complete?

588. Are Service Applications project team roles and responsibilities identified and documented?

589. Who is responsible for each task?

590. What is working well within your organizations performance management system?

591. To decide whether to use a quality measurement, ask how will you know when it is achieved?

592. Who: who is involved?

593. Implementation of actions: Who are the responsible units?

594. Have you ever been a part of this team?

595. What should you highlight for improvement?

596. Key conclusions and recommendations: Are conclusions and recommendations relevant and acceptable?

2.29 Human Resource Management Plan: Service Applications

597. Do Service Applications project teams & team members report on status / activities / progress?

598. Quality of people required to meet the forecast needs of the department?

599. Have Service Applications project success criteria been defined?

600. Quality assurance overheads?

601. Is there a Steering Committee in place?

602. Is there a Quality Management Plan?

603. Are post milestone Service Applications project reviews (PMPR) conducted with your organization at least once a year?

604. Has a structured approach been used to break work effort into manageable components (WBS)?

605. How does the proposed individual meet each requirement?

606. Are assumptions being identified, recorded, analyzed, qualified and closed?

607. Have the key elements of a coherent Service Applications project management strategy been

established?

608. Is the assigned Service Applications project manager a PMP (Certified Service Applications project manager) and experienced?

609. Have all documents been archived in a Service Applications project repository for each release?

610. Are trade-offs between accepting the risk and mitigating the risk identified?

611. Are quality inspections and review activities listed in the Service Applications project schedule(s)?

612. Does the schedule include Service Applications project management time and change request analysis time?

613. Is the current culture aligned with the vision, mission, and values of the department?

2.30 Communications Management Plan: Service Applications

614. How were corresponding initiatives successful?

615. Do you have members of your team responsible for certain stakeholders?

616. Can you think of other people who might have concerns or interests?

617. Which team member will work with each stakeholder?

618. Which stakeholders can influence others?

619. What communications method?

620. Who did you turn to if you had questions?

621. Who are the members of the governing body?

622. What to know?

623. Who will use or be affected by the result of a Service Applications project?

624. Who needs to know and how much?

625. Do you feel more overwhelmed by stakeholders?

626. Are the stakeholders getting the information others need, are others consulted, are concerns

addressed?

627. Do you then often overlook a key stakeholder or stakeholder group?

628. How do you manage communications?

629. What help do you and your team need from the stakeholder?

630. How is this initiative related to other portfolios, programs, or Service Applications projects?

631. Who were proponents/opponents?

632. Do you ask; can you recommend others for you to talk with about this initiative?

633. In your work, how much time is spent on stakeholder identification?

2.31 Risk Management Plan: Service Applications

634. Are status updates being made on schedule and are the updates clearly described?

635. Should the risk be taken at all?

636. What can you do to minimize the impact if it does?

637. What are the cost, schedule and resource impacts if the risk does occur?

638. Why do you need to manage Service Applications project Risk?

639. What other risks are created by choosing an avoidance strategy?

640. Monitoring -what factors can you track that will enable you to determine if the risk is becoming more or less likely?

641. Is the process supported by tools?

642. Which is an input to the risk management process?

643. Have top software and customer managers formally committed to support the Service Applications project?

644. Are the metrics meaningful and useful?

645. Was an original risk assessment/risk management plan completed?

646. Are certain activities taking a long time to complete?

647. What will the damage be?

648. Is a software Service Applications project management tool available?

649. Are you on schedule?

650. Are the reports useful and easy to read?

651. User involvement: do you have the right users?

2.32 Risk Register: Service Applications

652. Assume the risk event or situation happens, what would the impact be?

653. What will be done?

654. What should you do now?

655. What may happen or not go according to plan?

656. What is the reason for current performance gaps and do the risks and opportunities identified previously account for this?

657. Is further information required before making a decision?

658. Amongst the action plans and recommendations that you have to introduce are there some that could stop or delay the overall program?

659. Who needs to know about this?

660. What can be done about it?

661. Manageability – have mitigations to the risk been identified?

662. Are there other alternative controls that could be implemented?

663. What are your key risks/show istoppers and what is being done to manage them?

664. Which key risks have ineffective responses or outstanding improvement actions?

665. Who is accountable?

666. Does the evidence highlight any areas to advance opportunities or foster good relations. If yes what steps will be taken?

667. How are risks graded?

668. How often will the Risk Management Plan and Risk Register be formally reviewed, and by whom?

669. Do you require further engagement?

670. What is the probability and impact of the risk occurring?

2.33 Probability and Impact Assessment: Service Applications

671. How do you define a risk?

672. How would you suggest monitoring for risk transition indicators?

673. How are the local factors going to affect the absorption?

674. Can you avoid altogether some things that might go wrong?

675. What new technologies are being explored in the same area?

676. Have staff received necessary training?

677. What are the preparations required for facing difficulties?

678. What will be cost of redeployment of personnel?

679. Workarounds are determined during which step of risk management?

680. What should be the level of difficulty in handling the technology?

681. Do benefits and chances of success outweigh potential damage if success is not attained?

682. How would you assess the risk management process in the Service Applications project?

683. What risks are necessary to achieve success?

684. Assumptions analysis -what assumptions have you made or been given about your Service Applications project?

685. Is the customer willing to participate in reviews?

686. Monitoring of the overall Service Applications project status – are there any changes in the Service Applications project that can effect and cause new possible risks?

687. Is the technology to be built new to your organization?

688. Have top software and customer managers formally committed to support the Service Applications project?

689. Mitigation -how can you avoid the risk?

690. Are trained personnel, including supervisors and Service Applications project managers, available to handle such a large Service Applications project?

2.34 Probability and Impact Matrix: Service Applications

691. Can you handle the investment risk?

692. What can you use the analyzed risks for?

693. Are the risk data complete?

694. Management -what contingency plans do you have if the risk becomes a reality?

695. How are you working with risks?

696. Who are the owners?

697. Which is the BEST thing to do?

698. Could others have been better mitigated?

699. Is security a central objective?

700. How would you define a risk?

701. Pay attention to the quality of the plans: is the content complete, or does it seem to be lacking detail?

702. What is the likelihood of a breakthrough?

703. Does the software engineering team have the right mix of skills?

704. What are the chances the event will occur?

705. Is the present organizational structure for handling the Service Applications project sufficient?

706. What needs to be DONE?

707. What is the likely future demand of the customer?

708. Which phase of the Service Applications project do you take part in?

709. What kind of preparation would be required to do this?

2.35 Risk Data Sheet: Service Applications

710. What are your core values?

711. Is the data sufficiently specified in terms of the type of failure being analyzed, and its frequency or probability?

712. Risk of what?

713. If it happens, what are the consequences?

714. Has the most cost-effective solution been chosen?

715. What are the main threats to your existence?

716. How reliable is the data source?

717. How can it happen?

718. What are you here for (Mission)?

719. What if client refuses?

720. Type of risk identified?

721. What can you do?

722. What are you trying to achieve (Objectives)?

723. Are new hazards created?

724. Do effective diagnostic tests exist?

725. Potential for recurrence?

726. What is the chance that it will happen?

727. What are you weak at and therefore need to do better?

2.36 Procurement Management Plan: Service Applications

728. Published materials?

729. Is quality monitored from the perspective of the customers needs and expectations?

730. In which phase of the Acquisition Process Cycle does source qualifications reside?

731. Are corrective actions and variances reported?

732. Is there any form of automated support for Issues Management?

733. Are estimating assumptions and constraints captured?

734. Is there an on-going process in place to monitor Service Applications project risks?

735. Is there a procurement management plan in place?

736. Is there general agreement & acceptance of the current status and progress of the Service Applications project?

737. Are Service Applications project team members committed fulltime?

738. Has your organization readiness assessment

been conducted?

739. Are enough systems & user personnel assigned to the Service Applications project?

740. Is Service Applications project status reviewed with the steering and executive teams at appropriate intervals?

741. Similar Service Applications projects?

742. Are quality metrics defined?

2.37 Source Selection Criteria: Service Applications

743. What evidence should be provided regarding proposal evaluations?

744. Will the technical evaluation factor unnecessarily force the acquisition into a higher-priced market segment?

745. Have team members been adequately trained?

746. What are the guiding principles for developing an evaluation report?

747. What information may not be provided?

748. How should oral presentations be prepared for?

749. How do you encourage efficiency and consistency?

750. What should be considered?

751. What documentation should be used to support the selection decision?

752. What are the requirements for publicizing a RFP?

753. Is the offeror pricing what is technically proposed?

754. What is the effect of the debriefing schedule on

potential protests?

755. In order of importance, which evaluation criteria are the most critical to the determination of your overall rating?

756. What does a sample rating scale look like?

757. What will you use to capture evaluation and subsequent documentation?

758. Which contract type places the most risk on the seller?

759. Do you have a plan to document consensus results including disposition of any disagreement by individual evaluators?

760. When should debriefings be held and how should they be scheduled?

761. Have all evaluators been trained?

762. Who is on the Source Selection Advisory Committee?

2.38 Stakeholder Management Plan: Service Applications

763. Will all outputs delivered by the Service Applications project follow the same process?

764. Are tasks tracked by hours?

765. Who is responsible for the post implementation review process?

766. Where are the verification requirements to be documented (eg purchase order, agreement etc)?

767. Does the Service Applications project have a formal Service Applications project Charter?

768. Have all involved Service Applications project stakeholders and work groups committed to the Service Applications project?

769. Are written status reports provided on a designated frequent basis?

770. Have all necessary approvals been obtained?

771. Who would sign off on the charter?

772. Have Service Applications project management standards and procedures been identified / established and documented?

773. Is there an issues management plan in place?

774. Which of the records created within the Service Applications project, if any, does the Business Owner require access to?

775. How much information should be collected?

776. Who will be collecting information?

777. Have all stakeholders been identified?

778. Is the steering committee active in Service Applications project oversight?

779. Has a capability assessment been conducted?

2.39 Change Management Plan: Service Applications

780. What work practices will be affected?

781. Is there support for this application(s) and are the details available for distribution?

782. What goal(s) do you hope to accomplish?

783. Has this been negotiated with the customer and sponsor?

784. Is there a need for new relationships to be built?

785. What roles within your organization are affected, and how?

786. Impact of systems implementation on organization change?

787. Are there any restrictions on who can receive the communications?

788. Who might be able to help you the most?

789. Who will be the change levers?

790. Why is it important?

791. How prevalent is Resistance to Change?

792. Do the proposed users have access to the

appropriate documentation?

793. How much Service Applications project management is needed?

794. Is there an adequate supply of people for the new roles?

795. Is a training information sheet available?

796. What is the most positive interpretation it can receive?

797. What is going to be done differently?

798. What new behaviours are required?

3.0 Executing Process Group: Service Applications

799. How does Service Applications project management relate to other disciplines?

800. Why is it important to determine activity sequencing on Service Applications projects?

801. It under budget or over budget?

802. How well did the team follow the chosen processes?

803. Do the partners have sufficient financial capacity to keep up the benefits produced by the programme?

804. What are the challenges Service Applications project teams face?

805. What are the main types of goods and services being outsourced?

806. How could you control progress of your Service Applications project?

807. Would you rate yourself as being risk-averse, risk-neutral, or risk-seeking?

808. Are the necessary foundations in place to ensure the sustainability of the results of the programme?

809. Why do you need a good WBS to use Service

Applications project management software?

810. What areas does the group agree are the biggest success on the Service Applications project?

811. How well defined and documented were the Service Applications project management processes you chose to use?

812. Will additional funds be needed for hardware or software?

813. What is the difference between using brainstorming and the Delphi technique for risk identification?

814. What does it mean to take a systems view of a Service Applications project?

815. What good practices or successful experiences or transferable examples have been identified?

816. What type of information goes in the quality assurance plan?

3.1 Team Member Status Report: Service Applications

817. What specific interest groups do you have in place?

818. Is there evidence that staff is taking a more professional approach toward management of your organizations Service Applications projects?

819. Are the products of your organizations Service Applications projects meeting customers objectives?

820. How much risk is involved?

821. Why is it to be done?

822. How does this product, good, or service meet the needs of the Service Applications project and your organization as a whole?

823. The problem with Reward & Recognition Programs is that the truly deserving people all too often get left out. How can you make it practical?

824. How it is to be done?

825. Does the product, good, or service already exist within your organization?

826. Do you have an Enterprise Service Applications project Management Office (EPMO)?

827. Does your organization have the means (staff, money, contract, etc.) to produce or to acquire the product, good, or service?

828. Does every department have to have a Service Applications project Manager on staff?

829. Are the attitudes of staff regarding Service Applications project work improving?

830. Will the staff do training or is that done by a third party?

831. Are your organizations Service Applications projects more successful over time?

832. When a teams productivity and success depend on collaboration and the efficient flow of information, what generally fails them?

833. What is to be done?

834. How can you make it practical?

835. How will resource planning be done?

3.2 Change Request: Service Applications

836. What must be taken into consideration when introducing change control programs?

837. How is the change documented (format, content, storage)?

838. How are changes requested (forms, method of communication)?

839. What has an inspector to inspect and to check?

840. How fast will change requests be approved?

841. How are the measures for carrying out the change established?

842. Is it feasible to use requirements attributes as predictors of reliability?

843. Who has responsibility for approving and ranking changes?

844. How to get changes (code) out in a timely manner?

845. What is the function of the change control committee?

846. What mechanism is used to appraise others of changes that are made?

847. Who needs to approve change requests?

848. Where do changes come from?

849. How does a team identify the discrete elements of a configuration?

850. Who is responsible for the implementation and monitoring of all measures?

851. How do team members communicate with each other?

852. Should a more thorough impact analysis be conducted?

853. Customer acceptance plan how will the customer verify the change has been implemented successfully?

854. Will all change requests and current status be logged?

855. How does your organization control changes before and after software is released to a customer?

3.3 Change Log: Service Applications

856. How does this change affect scope?

857. Is the change request within Service Applications project scope?

858. Is the change backward compatible without limitations?

859. Is this a mandatory replacement?

860. Does the suggested change request represent a desired enhancement to the products functionality?

861. Will the Service Applications project fail if the change request is not executed?

862. Do the described changes impact on the integrity or security of the system?

863. Who initiated the change request?

864. How does this change affect the timeline of the schedule?

865. Is the requested change request a result of changes in other Service Applications project(s)?

866. Is the submitted change a new change or a modification of a previously approved change?

867. Is the change request open, closed or pending?

868. When was the request submitted?

869. When was the request approved?

870. How does this relate to the standards developed for specific business processes?

3.4 Decision Log: Service Applications

871. What alternatives/risks were considered?

872. Is your opponent open to a non-traditional workflow, or will it likely challenge anything you do?

873. Who will be given a copy of this document and where will it be kept?

874. Decision-making process; how will the team make decisions?

875. It becomes critical to track and periodically revisit both operational effectiveness; Are you noticing all that you need to, and are you interpreting what you see effectively?

876. Meeting purpose; why does this team meet?

877. How does provision of information, both in terms of content and presentation, influence acceptance of alternative strategies?

878. What makes you different or better than others companies selling the same thing?

879. Is everything working as expected?

880. With whom was the decision shared or considered?

881. How does an increasing emphasis on cost containment influence the strategies and tactics

used?

882. How do you know when you are achieving it?

883. How consolidated and comprehensive a story can you tell by capturing currently available incident data in a central location and through a log of key decisions during an incident?

884. What is your overall strategy for quality control / quality assurance procedures?

885. How does the use a Decision Support System influence the strategies/tactics or costs?

886. How do you define success?

887. Linked to original objective?

888. What are the cost implications?

889. Adversarial environment. is your opponent open to a non-traditional workflow, or will it likely challenge anything you do?

890. Behaviors; what are guidelines that the team has identified that will assist them with getting the most out of team meetings?

3.5 Quality Audit: Service Applications

891. Do the suppliers use a formal quality system?

892. How does your organization know that its system for supporting staff research capability is appropriately effective and constructive?

893. Are all areas associated with the storage and reconditioning of devices clean, free of rubbish, adequately ventilated and in good repair?

894. Is there a written corporate quality policy?

895. Is your organizational structure established and each positions responsibility defined?

896. How does your organization know that its relationships with relevant professional bodies are appropriately effective and constructive?

897. How does your organization know that its system for ensuring a positive organizational climate is appropriately effective and constructive?

898. What does an analysis of your organizations staff profile suggest in terms of its planning, and how is this being addressed?

899. Is the process of self review, learning and improvement endemic throughout your organization?

900. Is your organizations resource allocation system properly aligned with its collection of intentions?

901. How does your organization know that its research planning and management systems are appropriately effective and constructive in enabling quality research outcomes?

902. How does your organization know that its system for commercializing research outputs is appropriately effective and constructive?

903. Does everyone know what they are supposed to be doing, how and why?

904. Does your organization have set of goals, objectives, strategies and targets that are clearly understood by the Board and staff?

905. Are adequate and conveniently located toilet facilities available for use by the employees?

906. What mechanisms exist for identification of staff development needs?

907. How does your organization know that its methods are appropriately effective and constructive?

908. How does your organization know that its quality of teaching is appropriately effective and constructive?

909. How does your organization know that its staff are presenting original work, and properly acknowledging the work of others?

910. How does your organization know that the support for its staff is appropriately effective and constructive?

3.6 Team Directory: Service Applications

911. Process decisions: are all start-up, turn over and close out requirements of the contract satisfied?

912. Who are the Team Members?

913. Is construction on schedule?

914. How will you accomplish and manage the objectives?

915. Who will be the stakeholders on your next Service Applications project?

916. How will the team handle changes?

917. Process decisions: are there any statutory or regulatory issues relevant to the timely execution of work?

918. What are you going to deliver or accomplish?

919. When will you produce deliverables?

920. Who will talk to the customer?

921. How do unidentified risks impact the outcome of the Service Applications project?

922. Where will the product be used and/or delivered or built when appropriate?

923. Why is the work necessary?

924. Decisions: is the most suitable form of contract being used?

925. How and in what format should information be presented?

926. Process decisions: is work progressing on schedule and per contract requirements?

927. How does the team resolve conflicts and ensure tasks are completed?

928. Process decisions: are contractors adequately prosecuting the work?

929. Who will write the meeting minutes and distribute?

930. Timing: when do the effects of communication take place?

3.7 Team Operating Agreement: Service Applications

931. What individual strengths does each team member bring to the group?

932. Do you ask participants to close laptops and place mobile devices on silent on the table while the meeting is in progress?

933. Are leadership responsibilities shared among team members (versus a single leader)?

934. Did you determine the technology methods that best match the messages to be communicated?

935. Must your team members rely on the expertise of other members to complete tasks?

936. Did you recap the meeting purpose, time, and expectations?

937. What is the anticipated procedure (recruitment, solicitation of volunteers, or assignment) for selecting team members?

938. Do you post meeting notes and the recording (if used) and notify participants?

939. How will you divide work equitably?

940. Do team members need to frequently communicate as a full group to make timely

decisions?

941. Do you brief absent members after they view meeting notes or listen to a recording?

942. What is teaming?

943. What are the current caseload numbers in the unit?

944. Did you prepare participants for the next meeting?

945. Do you solicit member feedback about meetings and what would make them better?

946. Seconds for members to respond?

947. Have you set the goals and objectives of the team?

948. To whom do you deliver your services?

949. What is culture?

950. Reimbursements: how will the team members be reimbursed for expenses and time commitments?

3.8 Team Performance Assessment: Service Applications

951. What do you think is the most constructive thing that could be done now to resolve considerations and disputes about method variance?

952. To what degree are staff involved as partners in the improvement process?

953. To what degree do all members feel responsible for all agreed-upon measures?

954. Do friends perform better than acquaintances?

955. Do you promptly inform members about major developments that may affect them?

956. To what degree do members understand and articulate the same purpose without relying on ambiguous abstractions?

957. To what degree do team members frequently explore the teams purpose and its implications?

958. Social categorization and intergroup behaviour: Does minimal intergroup discrimination make social identity more positive?

959. To what degree does the teams approach to its work allow for modification and improvement over time?

960. When does the medium matter?

961. Can team performance be reliably measured in simulator and live exercises using the same assessment tool?

962. To what degree does the teams purpose constitute a broader, deeper aspiration than just accomplishing short-term goals?

963. To what degree will the team adopt a concrete, clearly understood, and agreed-upon approach that will result in achievement of the teams goals?

964. To what degree can all members engage in open and interactive considerations?

965. To what degree do team members understand one anothers roles and skills?

966. To what degree do members articulate the goals beyond the team membership?

967. To what degree are the goals ambitious?

968. To what degree are the members clear on what they are individually responsible for and what they are jointly responsible for?

969. Which situations call for a more extreme type of adaptiveness in which team members actually re-define roles?

970. Lack of method variance in self-reported affect and perceptions at work: Reality or artifact?

3.9 Team Member Performance Assessment: Service Applications

971. Why do performance reviews?

972. What, if any, steps are available for employees who feel they have been unfairly or inaccurately rated?

973. In what areas would you like to concentrate your knowledge and resources?

974. How are training activities developed from a technical perspective?

975. Do the goals support your organizations goals?

976. Does the rater (supervisor) have the authority or responsibility to tell an employee that the employees performance is unsatisfactory?

977. What is a significant fact or event?

978. What happens if a team member disagrees with the Job Expectations?

979. Are the draft goals SMART ?

980. What future plans (e.g., modifications) do you have for your program?

981. How do you currently use the time that is available?

982. For what period of time is a member rated?

983. How often should assessments be conducted?

984. How is your organizations Strategic Management System tied to performance measurement?

985. How do you implement Cost Reduction?

986. What is a general description of the processes under performance measurement and assessment?

987. What are the basic principles and objectives of performance measurement and assessment?

988. What are the standards or expectations for success?

3.10 Issue Log: Service Applications

989. Who is the stakeholder?

990. Why do you manage communications?

991. Do you prepare stakeholder engagement plans?

992. Are there too many who have an interest in some aspect of your work?

993. Are there potential barriers between the team and the stakeholder?

994. How do you manage human resources?

995. What are the typical contents?

996. What are the stakeholders interrelationships?

997. Is the issue log kept in a safe place?

998. What is the impact on the Business Case?

999. What effort will a change need?

1000. Who reported the issue?

1001. How much time does it take to do it?

1002. Are stakeholder roles recognized by your organization?

1003. Can an impact cause deviation beyond team,

stage or Service Applications project tolerances?

1004. Are the Service Applications project issues uniquely identified, including to which product they refer?

1005. Which stakeholders are thought leaders, influences, or early adopters?

4.0 Monitoring and Controlling Process Group: Service Applications

1006. How many potential communications channels exist on the Service Applications project?

1007. How to ensure validity, quality and consistency?

1008. Use: how will they use the information?

1009. How are you doing?

1010. How many more potential communications channels were introduced by the discovery of the new stakeholders?

1011. How were collaborations developed, and how are they sustained?

1012. How well did you do?

1013. What areas does the group agree are the biggest success on the Service Applications project?

1014. What resources (both financial and non-financial) are available/needed?

1015. What areas were overlooked on this Service Applications project?

1016. How is agile program management done?

1017. Is it what was agreed upon?

1018. Is the verbiage used appropriate and understandable?

1019. What are the goals of the program?

1020. How well did the chosen processes fit the needs of the Service Applications project?

1021. How was the program set-up initiated?

4.1 Project Performance Report: Service Applications

1022. Next Steps?

1023. To what degree does the teams work approach provide opportunity for members to engage in fact-based problem solving?

1024. To what degree do team members articulate the teams work approach?

1025. To what degree is there centralized control of information sharing?

1026. To what degree will team members, individually and collectively, commit time to help themselves and others learn and develop skills?

1027. To what degree is there a sense that only the team can succeed?

1028. To what degree will the approach capitalize on and enhance the skills of all team members in a manner that takes into consideration other demands on members of the team?

1029. To what degree can team members meet frequently enough to accomplish the teams ends?

1030. What is in it for you?

1031. To what degree will each member have the

opportunity to advance his or her professional skills in all three of the above categories while contributing to the accomplishment of the teams purpose and goals?

1032. What is the degree to which rules govern information exchange between individuals within your organization?

1033. To what degree are fresh input and perspectives systematically caught and added (for example, through information and analysis, new members, and senior sponsors)?

1034. To what degree does the information network communicate information relevant to the task?

1035. To what degree does the team possess adequate membership to achieve its ends?

1036. To what degree does the teams work approach provide opportunity for members to engage in open interaction?

1037. To what degree do team members agree with the goals, relative importance, and the ways in which achievement will be measured?

1038. To what degree do the structures of the formal organization motivate taskrelevant behavior and facilitate task completion?

4.2 Variance Analysis: Service Applications

1039. Are meaningful indicators identified for use in measuring the status of cost and schedule performance?

1040. Contemplated overhead expenditure for each period based on the best information currently is available?

1041. How does your organization allocate the cost of shared expenses and services?

1042. Are your organizations and items of cost assigned to each pool identified?

1043. When, during the last four quarters, did a primary business event occur causing a fluctuation?

1044. What are the direct labor dollars and/or hours?

1045. What is the performance to date and material commitment?

1046. What causes selling price variance?

1047. Who is generally responsible for monitoring and taking action on variances?

1048. Are records maintained to show how management reserves are used?

1049. Favorable or unfavorable variance?

1050. How do you verify authorization to proceed with all authorized work?

1051. How does the monthly budget compare to the actual experience?

1052. Did an existing competitor change strategy?

1053. Is the anticipated (firm and potential) business base Service Applications projected in a rational, consistent manner?

1054. Who are responsible for the establishment of budgets and assignment of resources for overhead performance?

1055. Are there knowledgeable Service Applications projections of future performance?

1056. Why do variances exist?

4.3 Earned Value Status: Service Applications

1057. Validation is a process of ensuring that the developed system will actually achieve the stakeholders desired outcomes; Are you building the right product? What do you validate?

1058. Are you hitting your Service Applications projects targets?

1059. How does this compare with other Service Applications projects?

1060. Where is evidence-based earned value in your organization reported?

1061. Where are your problem areas?

1062. How much is it going to cost by the finish?

1063. Verification is a process of ensuring that the developed system satisfies the stakeholders agreements and specifications; Are you building the product right? What do you verify?

1064. Earned value can be used in almost any Service Applications project situation and in almost any Service Applications project environment. it may be used on large Service Applications projects, medium sized Service Applications projects, tiny Service Applications projects (in cut-down form), complex and simple Service Applications projects and in any market sector. some people, of course, know all about earned value, they have used it for years - but perhaps not as effectively as they could have?

1065. If earned value management (EVM) is so good in determining the true status of a Service Applications project and Service Applications project its completion, why is it that hardly any one uses it in information systems related Service Applications projects?

1066. When is it going to finish?

1067. What is the unit of forecast value?

4.4 Risk Audit: Service Applications

1068. Where will the next scandal or adverse media involving your organization come from?

1069. What are the Internal Controls ?

1070. Is a software Service Applications project management tool available?

1071. When your organization is entering into a major contract, does it seek legal advice?

1072. How do you manage risk?

1073. What are risks and how do you manage them?

1074. Do you have a consistent repeatable process that is actually used?

1075. What are the legal implications of not identifying a complete universe of business risks?

1076. Have you considered the health and safety of everyone in your organization and do you meet work health and safety regulations?

1077. Does willful intent modify risk-based auditing?

1078. Are formal technical reviews part of this process?

1079. How do you prioritize risks?

1080. Are staff committed for the duration of the product?

1081. Do you have a procedure for dealing with complaints?

1082. What effect would a better risk management program have had?

1083. Are the software tools integrated with each other?

1084. Do you have a clear plan for the future that describes what you want to do and how you are going to do it?

1085. Is your organization an exempt employer for payroll tax purposes?

1086. Are audit program plans risk-adjusted?

1087. Level of preparation and skill?

4.5 Contractor Status Report: Service Applications

1088. How long have you been using the services?

1089. What is the average response time for answering a support call?

1090. Are there contractual transfer concerns?

1091. What process manages the contracts?

1092. What was the budget or estimated cost for your organizations services?

1093. If applicable; describe your standard schedule for new software version releases. Are new software version releases included in the standard maintenance plan?

1094. What are the minimum and optimal bandwidth requirements for the proposed solution?

1095. How is risk transferred?

1096. Describe how often regular updates are made to the proposed solution. Are corresponding regular updates included in the standard maintenance plan?

1097. Who can list a Service Applications project as organization experience, your organization or a previous employee of your organization?

1098. What was the actual budget or estimated cost for your organizations services?

1099. What was the overall budget or estimated cost?

1100. What was the final actual cost?

4.6 Formal Acceptance: Service Applications

1101. General estimate of the costs and times to complete the Service Applications project?

1102. What is the Acceptance Management Process?

1103. Is formal acceptance of the Service Applications project product documented and distributed?

1104. Was the Service Applications project goal achieved?

1105. What lessons were learned about your Service Applications project management methodology?

1106. Was the Service Applications project managed well?

1107. What are the requirements against which to test, Who will execute?

1108. How does your team plan to obtain formal acceptance on your Service Applications project?

1109. What features, practices, and processes proved to be strengths or weaknesses?

1110. Do you buy pre-configured systems or build your own configuration?

1111. Did the Service Applications project achieve its

MOV?

1112. What function(s) does it fill or meet?

1113. How well did the team follow the methodology?

1114. Does it do what Service Applications project team said it would?

1115. Did the Service Applications project manager and team act in a professional and ethical manner?

1116. Do you buy-in installation services?

1117. Who supplies data?

1118. Was the sponsor/customer satisfied?

1119. Do you perform formal acceptance or burn-in tests?

1120. Have all comments been addressed?

5.0 Closing Process Group: Service Applications

1121. What were things that you need to improve?

1122. Are there funding or time constraints?

1123. What were the desired outcomes?

1124. What could have been improved?

1125. Is there a clear cause and effect between the activity and the lesson learned?

1126. Will the Service Applications project deliverable(s) replace a current asset or group of assets?

1127. Did you do what you said you were going to do?

1128. Were cost budgets met?

1129. What is the risk of failure to your organization?

1130. What business situation is being addressed?

1131. If action is called for, what form should it take?

1132. What areas were overlooked on this Service Applications project?

1133. How dependent is the Service Applications project on other Service Applications projects or work efforts?

1134. How well defined and documented were the Service Applications project management processes you chose to use?

1135. Did the delivered product meet the specified requirements and goals of the Service Applications project?

1136. Were risks identified and mitigated?

1137. Mitigate. what will you do to minimize the impact should a risk event occur?

5.1 Procurement Audit: Service Applications

1138. How do you address the risk of fraud and corruption?

1139. Are there policies regarding special approval for capital expenditures?

1140. Are all purchase orders signed by the purchasing agent?

1141. Are checks used in numeric sequence?

1142. Could bidders learn all relevant information straight from the tender documents?

1143. Did the conditions of contract comply with the detail provided in the procurement documents and with the outcome of the procurement procedure followed?

1144. Is there a practice that prohibits signing blank purchase orders?

1145. Are there mechanisms for evaluating the departments suppliers performance in relation to prices, quality, delivery and innovation?

1146. Is there a policy covering the relationship of other departments with vendors?

1147. Must the receipt of goods be approved prior to

payment?

1148. Has an upper limit of cost been fixed?

1149. Is a physical inventory taken periodically to verify fixed asset records?

1150. Is there ineffective internal communication in the procurement function/unit?

1151. Are periodic audits made of disbursement activities?

1152. Are there procedures to ensure that changes to purchase orders will be updated on the computer files?

1153. Are unusual uses of organization funds investigated?

1154. Were bids properly evaluated?

1155. Does each policy statement contain the legal reference(s) on which the policy is based?

1156. Does the procurement function/unit have the ability to secure best performance from contractors?

1157. Does your organization have an overall procurement strategy and/or policy?

5.2 Contract Close-Out: Service Applications

1158. What is capture management?

1159. Have all acceptance criteria been met prior to final payment to contractors?

1160. Was the contract sufficiently clear so as not to result in numerous disputes and misunderstandings?

1161. Are the signers the authorized officials?

1162. Was the contract type appropriate?

1163. Have all contracts been closed?

1164. What happens to the recipient of services?

1165. Change in circumstances?

1166. Parties: Authorized?

1167. Change in attitude or behavior?

1168. How is the contracting office notified of the automatic contract close-out?

1169. How/when used ?

1170. Have all contracts been completed?

1171. How does it work?

1172. Change in knowledge?

1173. Have all contract records been included in the Service Applications project archives?

1174. Was the contract complete without requiring numerous changes and revisions?

1175. Has each contract been audited to verify acceptance and delivery?

1176. Parties: who is involved?

5.3 Project or Phase Close-Out: Service Applications

1177. Does the lesson educate others to improve performance?

1178. Were messages directly related to the release strategy or phases of the Service Applications project?

1179. What stakeholder group needs, expectations, and interests are being met by the Service Applications project?

1180. How often did each stakeholder need an update?

1181. What could be done to improve the process?

1182. Who controlled the resources for the Service Applications project?

1183. Who are the Service Applications project stakeholders and what are roles and involvement?

1184. Can the lesson learned be replicated?

1185. What were the actual outcomes?

1186. What are the informational communication needs for each stakeholder?

1187. What process was planned for managing issues/risks?

1188. What is a Risk?

1189. What is this stakeholder expecting?

1190. What was expected from each stakeholder?

1191. What can you do better next time, and what specific actions can you take to improve?

1192. What is a Risk Management Process?

1193. What are they?

5.4 Lessons Learned: Service Applications

1194. What is the impact of tax policy?

1195. What are the conceptual limits of the research?

1196. How effective was the quality assurance process?

1197. Was the Service Applications project significantly delayed/hampered by outside dependencies (outside to the Service Applications project, that is)?

1198. How well prepared were you to receive Service Applications project deliverables?

1199. What rewards do the individuals seek?

1200. What is the supplier dependency?

1201. What is the desired end-state?

1202. To what extent was the evolution of risks communicated?

1203. What is the economic growth rate?

1204. How often do communications get lost?

1205. What is the distribution of authority?

1206. How efficient and effective were Service Applications project team meetings?

1207. How well do you feel the executives supported this Service Applications project?

1208. How well were expectations met regarding the frequency and content of information that was conveyed to by the Service Applications project Manager?

1209. Are the lessons more complex and multivariate?

1210. How accurately and timely was the Risk Management Log updated or reviewed?

1211. What was the methodology behind successful learning experiences, and how might they be applied to the broader challenge of your organizations knowledge management?

1212. How effectively and consistently was sponsorship for the Service Applications project conveyed?

1213. What is your working hypothesis, if you have one?

Index

management 1, 3-5, 8-9, 19, 22, 32, 41, 44, 58-59, 63-64, 68, 72, 78-80, 85, 87, 89, 113, 124, 127, 132-133, 135, 137, 139, 145, 152, 154, 158, 169-170, 172, 174-175, 181-182, 186, 191-194, 196-197, 199-202, 206, 210, 212-216, 225, 234, 237, 241, 244-246, 249, 252, 255, 258, 260
manager   7, 9, 31, 36, 135, 137, 145, 168, 174, 188, 193, 217, 250, 260
managers   2, 125, 168, 196, 201
manages   79, 128, 247
managing   2, 86, 125, 130, 257
mandatory   220
manner   17, 79, 126, 218, 239, 242, 250
mantle 108
Mapping   61, 63, 70
marked   146
market 15, 208, 244
marketer   7
Marketing   116
markets   25
Master 173
material   152, 185, 189, 241
materials   1, 206
matrices   143
Matrix 2-5, 131, 143, 188, 202
matter 28, 43, 49, 232
maximizing 119
meaning   158
meaningful 55, 111, 151, 197, 241
measurable 39-40, 129, 177
measure   2, 9, 21, 24, 34, 37, 43-45, 48, 50-54, 60, 65, 74, 76-77, 88, 92, 95-96, 98, 128, 132-133, 178
measured   19, 46, 49-50, 52-55, 57, 80, 98, 100, 184-185, 232, 240
measures   46-51, 65, 68-69, 88, 91, 93-94, 134, 218-219, 231
measuring   93, 241
mechanical 1
mechanism   147, 218
mechanisms 187, 225, 253
medium   232, 243
meeting   34, 39, 100, 154, 190, 216, 222, 228-230
meetings   33, 40, 174, 223, 230, 260
megatrends 116

prevent 54
prevents 18
previous 41, 160, 172, 247
previously 198, 220
prices 253
pricing 208
primary 52, 139, 166, 241
principles 135, 154, 208, 234
priorities 44, 48, 55, 180
prioritize 182, 188, 245
priority 45, 50
privacy 30, 184
problem 15-16, 18-21, 23-25, 27, 29, 39, 41, 54-55, 62, 72, 139, 142, 216, 239, 243
problems 16, 19-22, 24, 79, 82, 101, 134, 141
procedure 152, 229, 246, 253
procedures 9, 86, 93, 95-96, 99, 138, 155, 164, 169, 172, 182, 184, 187, 210, 223, 254
proceed 242
proceeding 173
process 1-7, 9, 29, 34-37, 39, 42, 56, 58-62, 64-72, 74, 88, 91, 93-98, 100, 126, 129, 133, 139-143, 145-148, 154, 164, 168-169, 171, 174-175, 183, 186, 196, 201, 206, 210, 214, 222, 224, 227-228, 231, 237, 243, 245, 247, 249, 251, 257-259
processes 50, 56, 61, 63-69, 71, 90, 93, 96, 126-127, 133, 146, 148, 151, 183, 187, 214-215, 221, 234, 238, 249, 252
produce 59, 164, 217, 227
produced 70, 80, 145, 214
producing 143
product 1, 47, 69, 107, 117, 138-139, 148, 160, 180-181, 185, 216-217, 227, 236, 243, 246, 249, 252
production 30, 87, 105, 131
products 1, 22, 26, 47, 103, 119, 140, 143, 151, 176, 216, 220
profile 224
program 24, 48, 59, 100, 133, 182, 190, 198, 233, 237-238, 246
programme 214
programs 195, 216, 218
progress 30, 50, 76, 95, 107, 122, 128, 131, 178, 186, 192, 206, 214, 229
prohibited 152
prohibits 253

remember 171
remunerate 78
repair 224
repeatable 245
rephrased 9
replace 51, 251
replaced 134
replanning 152
replicated 257
Report 5-6, 88, 93, 161, 192, 208, 216, 239, 247
reported 152, 184, 189, 206, 235, 243
reporting 64, 99, 112, 189
reports 53, 99, 130, 135, 145, 197, 210
repository 154, 193
represent 80, 180, 220
reproduced 1
request 5, 62, 180, 193, 218, 220-221
requested 1, 83, 218, 220
requests 218-219
require 28, 44, 66, 93, 164, 199, 211
required 21, 26, 29-31, 33, 35, 46, 63, 67, 80, 83, 94, 126, 133, 142, 156, 166, 192, 198, 200, 203, 213
requiring 130, 256
research 15, 102, 117, 161, 168, 224-225, 259
reserve 152
reserved 1
reserves 138, 241
reside 87, 206
Resistance 212
resolution 72, 87
resolve 19-21, 228, 231
resolved 185
resource 3-4, 115, 134, 138, 159, 164, 166-167, 192, 196, 217, 225
resources 2, 7, 19, 23-25, 34, 37-38, 56, 67, 80, 91, 94, 98, 104, 115, 117, 126-127, 129, 154, 156, 158-159, 162, 166-167, 170, 179-180, 233, 235, 237, 242, 257
respect 1
respond 134, 230
responded 11
response 15, 24, 91-92, 97-98, 101, 247
responses 84, 199
responsive 170, 178